HOW TO TRAIN A
SUPERDOG

HOW TO TRAIN A
SUPERDOG

GWEN **BAILEY**

LONDON, NEW YORK, MELBOURNE, MUNICH, AND DELHI

Project Art Editor
Francis Wong

Project Editor
Victoria Wiggins

Designers
Peter Laws, Steve Woosnam-Savage

Editors
Jamie Ambrose, Steve Setford, Heather Thomas, Rebecca Warren

Design Assistant
Rebecca Tennant

Editorial Assistants
Lizzie Munsey, Jaime Tenreiro

Production
Rebecca Short

Production Editor
Maria Elia

Jacket Designer
Duncan Turner

Managing Editor
Sarah Larter

Managing Art Editor
Phil Ormerod

Publishing Manager
Liz Wheeler

Art Director
Bryn Walls

Publisher
Jonathan Metcalf

Art Direction
Bev Speight, Nigel Wright
XAB Design

Photographer
Gerard Brown

Published in Great Britain in 2009
By Dorling Kindersley Limited 80 Strand, London WC2R ORL

A Penguin Company
Copyright © 2009 Dorling Kindersley Limited
Text copyright © Gwen Bailey

2 4 6 8 10 9 7 5 3 1

A CIP catalogue record for this book is available from the British Library

ISBN 978 1 4053 3234 7

Colour reproduction by Alta Images, Colourscan
Printed and bound by Star Standard, Singapore

See our complete catalogue at
www.dk.com

Disclaimer

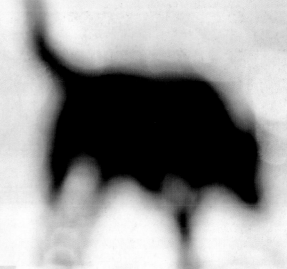

Contents

∨ Loving relationship
Dogs are social animals, and building a relationship with your dog, based on love, trust, and respect, is the essential foundation for positive training.

△ Holding the future
Puppies are delightful, but need lots of care. Habits learned in puppyhood will last a lifetime. Owners are solely responsible for their good education.

△ Essential lessons
Training your dog to come back when you call, sit when asked, and walk on a loose lead will make walks more pleasant and safer.

Introduction

Many owners dream of a owning a happy, outgoing dog that does everything they ask, never makes a wrong move, and seems to know their every thought.

Well, your dog can be like this too. It takes effort and knowledge, but all the knowledge you need is in this book. Dogs are living, thinking beings with adaptable brains that can be reprogrammed into good habits. You just have to know how to do it, and here you will find all the information you need.

Whether you already own a dog, or are about to acquire a new adult dog or puppy, this book will help you to bring out the best in him and maximize the benefits of ownership. Just like an operating manual for a car or washing machine, here are the operating instructions for your dog. They may seem complex, but the exercises in this book are designed to be easy at first, progressing through to more difficult training later as you develop your skills.

Further, this book tells you how to develop a good working relationship with your dog, based on love and respect. It also gives you the necessary guidance to develop an

▽ Clever dog
Teaching your dog to find lost keys takes patience and skill, but it is an easy exercise for dogs, with their amazing sense of smell.

△ Taking the lead
Leadership and respect are key qualities for an owner. Respect can't be gained by intimidation, but is earned by taking control of events and making good decisions.

▽ Contented life
A dog that has all of his psychological and physical needs met will be happy and relaxed. A fulfilled dog is more likely to live a long, healthy life.

Dogs that can help you with household chores can be closely involved with your life. This gives them purpose and helps dogs from working stock to feel fulfilled.

△ **Fun times**
Teaching fun tricks and exercises will give your dog an outlet for his mental energy, as well as providing him with a way to entertain you and your friends.

△ **Play energy**
Dogs love to play and it is essential that owners provide an outlet, in the form of games with toys, to help use up playful energy.

▽ Self-control
Learning to wait for things you want is an important lesson for dogs. Those that learn self-control will be much nicer to live with.

▽ Willing partner
Building a strong working relationship with your dog and teaching him a range of cues for a variety of actions will result in a willing friend and partner.

△ Sporting activities
Canine sports are entertaining for both dogs and owners. They bring the challenge of learning new skills and enable you to meet new people and other dogs.

The **right dog** for **you**

1

Choosing a dog

Choosing a dog

Choosing a new dog is **exciting** and **emotional.** We are all prone to choosing what looks familiar and attractive, whether it suits us or not. Making the **right choice** is more likely, however, if you take time to consider **temperament and characteristics,** and think carefully about what kind of dog will complement your own personality. This section will help you to do that, explaining why **different breeds** have **different behaviour traits** as well as physical forms, so that you can find a breed that will **fit into your lifestyle.** It will also help you decide whether a **puppy or** an **adult** may be more suitable, and will **enable** you to **find** a **dog** that is **just right for you.**

ACTIVE DOGS
If you choose an energetic dog, you need to be prepared to be active yourself if you are to have a happy life together.

Choosing a dog

Thinking carefully about your expectations and requirements before you select a dog will help you to choose one with the right temperament that suits you well and fits easily into your lifestyle and daily routine.

Examine your lifestyle

Dogs come in all shapes and sizes, and there are numerous breeds and different types of character from which to choose. To make selecting a dog easier, you should think very carefully about what you and your family really want from owning one. To begin this selection process, consider your requirements under the following headings:

How much time do you have?
Think honestly about whether you have sufficient time for playing games with a dog, exercising and grooming him, giving him love and attention, plus the extra time that will be needed for keeping your house clean, as even the cleanest dog brings in dirt and makes a lot of mess. Do you have enough spare time every day for owning a dog?

How much are you at home? If you add up the hours you spend at home during an average week, you may find that your lifestyle is not suited to owning a dog that needs many hours of companionship each day.

How much can you afford? Bigger dogs cost more to feed than small ones, but all dogs need veterinary care as well as health insurance. Some pet insurance companies offer a reduced rate for non-

△ **Energetic dogs**
Dogs with naturally high energy levels need energetic owners who enjoy exercising with them on a daily basis. Providing the right amount of exercise will result in a contented dog.

◁ **Happy families**
Fun-loving, sociable dogs, such as spaniels, make playful pets. Choosing a dog that fits into your home easily and matches your expectations will take some research, but it will result in a happy dog and a contented family.

pedigree dogs. Dogs with coats that need clipping or stripping require frequent visits to the local grooming parlour. Can you afford all these costs of dog ownership?

How active are you? Getting an active dog with lots of energy is not a wise decision if you are a couch potato who likes nothing better than to relax in front of the television all evening and much of the weekend. All dogs need daily exercise.

What "personality" and character traits does your ideal dog have? Once you have decided what you want from a dog, sourcing the right dog for you becomes easier. Finding out what different dog breeds need in terms of their physical requirements, assessing their character type to see if it fits in with yours, and seeing if their needs match what you can provide are quite easy. Take care to research all these issues thoroughly in advance.

Selecting by temperament

Many people choose their dog by browsing through breed books and finding one they like the look of. This dog will often appear familiar, resembling a previously owned pet, or may even have quite similar facial characteristics to themselves. Choosing by looks alone without considering the behaviour traits and character type of that breed can be a mistake, and new owners may end up with a dog who does not suit them in fundamental ways. Choosing by temperament is a much better way to select a dog.

> **"To make** the process of **selection easier,** you should **think very carefully about** what you and your family **want from a dog."**

Does the dog have to be good with others? Do you have children, a baby (or perhaps you are planning to have one in the future), elderly relatives, other dogs, or small pets? A new dog in your home will have an impact on everyone in your family and he needs to be able to get on with others. Consider his effect on existing relationships.

Adult or puppy? You also need to decide whether to get an adult dog or a puppy. Puppies are a clean slate and they are relatively easy to mould to your ways, although you need to make sure that you find a healthy, well-socialized one whose parents and grandparents have a good temperament. Puppies are lovely, but they do need an

intensive period of training and education, as well as a large amount of your time in their first year to help them develop into perfect pets.

Adult dogs are already formed, and the difficult house-training, chewing, and the early education stages are all over. They are ready-made dogs and what you see is what you get, although they will eventually adapt to your ways and routine with some careful education. However, you must take time to get to know them before you decide.

◁ **Time consuming**
Puppies are delightful but, until mature, they require constant care and attention for essential socialization, training, education, and companionship. Only consider owning one if you have the time.

Where to **find your dog**

Many different places can supply adult dogs and puppies, but not all are reputable, so make sure you use a reliable source. Take care to choose a healthy animal with the right temperament for you and your family.

Finding the right dog for you can take time, and it requires careful searching. It is easy to fall in love with the first dog or puppy you see, but avoid making a hasty choice – you will be spending many years together, so it is worth being patient and hanging on until you find exactly what you are looking for.

Adult dogs

The best source of adult dogs is a reputable rescue centre that carefully assesses the dogs it puts up for adoption. Assessment is difficult, because a dog's behaviour changes when it enters kennels, and staff have to predict what it will be like in a home environment.

Instead of kennels, some rescue centres place all their dogs with foster carers. These temporary owners learn a lot about the dog in the real-life situation of a home, and they can usually give you a very clear picture of what you can expect from the dog when it comes to your house to live with you.

As well as rescue organizations that cater for all breeds and crossbreeds, some specialist rescue centres concentrate on a single breed. If you know what breed you want, this may be a good place to source your dog.

Breeders sometimes advertise adult dogs. Beware kennel-raised dogs, as they rarely make successful pets.

▽ **Get to know him**
At the rescue centre, spend some time getting to know a new dog before deciding, as this may reveal unwanted traits or could confirm that he is the right dog for you.

△ **The right dog**
A good rescue centre will assess the dogs in their care before putting them up for adoption, making it easier to choose one who is right for you. Don't be tempted to take home the first appealing dog you see.

▷ **Be prepared**
You should be prepared for the rescue centre to assess your suitability as an owner. They may want to meet all your family and ask some personal questions about your home, work, and lifestyle.

△ **The right environment**
Always ask to see the puppies with their mother, and check that she is friendly. The "nest area" should be clean, with a larger "toileting area" that is lined with sheets of newspaper.

▷ **Pleased to meet you**
Well-socialized puppies should be interested in strangers and happy to see them. Avoid any who are nervous, move away, or are more interested in playing with each other than meeting you.

Acquiring an adult dog via a newspaper advertisement is not advisable, as you will only have a limited time to get to know the dog. What's more, you may not be told the truth about the dog's history, and you may be put under pressure to take the dog immediately.

Puppies

Finding a breeder who produces healthy, well-socialized dogs with good temperaments is difficult. Research the breeder's reputation, and come away without a puppy if you do not like what you see. Check that the puppy has been reared at home, and not just brought into the house for your visit. Be suspicious of large kennels where many puppies are produced and little effort is put into socializing, particularly if the emphasis is on winning show prizes.

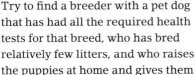

Try to find a breeder with a pet dog that has had all the required health tests for that breed, who has bred relatively few litters, and who raises the puppies at home and gives them all the socialization and habituation they need to grow into well-adjusted adult dogs. When choosing, go for puppies that show an interest in you and readily come to greet you.

> "It is worth **being patient** and **hanging on** until you find **exactly** what you are **looking for.**"

Sources to avoid

Never buy a puppy if you cannot see the conditions in which it was raised or meet its mother, or if it has been kept in a kennel, barn, outhouse, or stable. Steer clear of pet shops, and breeders who want to exchange puppies for cash at the roadside. Avoid outlets selling many different breeds, because they may obtain dogs from places where they are farmed. The puppies may look normal, but they often have health problems and poor temperaments.

The **wolf within**

Domestic dogs are descendants of the Grey Wolf (*Canis lupus*). Although they are very different from their predecessors, many traits have been retained, and selective breeding has accentuated those we find useful.

Teamwork

Grey Wolves, the ancestors of all pet and working dogs, have evolved into cooperative hunters of large prey. Although they will catch small animals, including mice, rabbits, and even fish, they are capable of working together as a pack to bring down much bigger prey, such as deer, moose, elk, and caribou.

In order to hunt as a team, wolves need to live together to build up and maintain bonds between them. As a result, they need to be social and cooperative. These are the traits that make domestic dogs so successful as workers and pets.

Wolf becomes dog

There are many theories as to how wolves became domesticated, the most probable being that dogs evolved over many generations from wolves that lived at the edges of human settlements, on the waste dumps of villages. Over the years,

▷ **Ancestors**
Intelligent and resourceful, the Grey Wolf is very different from the domestic dog, but has passed many character traits down to our pets.

Tracking   Watching   Chasing

> **"Dogs evolved** over many generations **from wolves** that lived at the **edges of human settlements,** on the **waste dumps** of villages."

those with the least fearful genes thrived alongside people, and they gradually became a distinct species. They probably closely resembled the village dogs that can be seen in many developing countries today.

Selective breeding

From these first village dogs, we have gradually developed all the different types and breeds that exist today, using a technique known as selective breeding. This involves breeding only from the dogs that have the particular traits desired. To assist them in a range of tasks, breeders selected for various parts of the dogs' hunting sequence (below). For example, to produce dogs that were efficient vermin hunters, the "catch and kill" part of this behavioural sequence was required, and dogs that proved to be good at this were selected for breeding. To develop good herding dogs, breeders chose dogs that excelled at the chase element of the hunting sequence, producing a dog that loved to chase but without the Terrier's strong desire to catch and

▷ ▽ **Different forms**
Domestic dogs look very different to their ancestors, and behave very differently too. Their bodies have been transformed to suit the work they were bred for, so that all sorts of shapes, sizes, colours, and coat types are available. Likewise, their character traits and propensities for different behaviours have been altered to produce a variety of attitudes and characters.

kill. As well as producing dogs with different behavioural traits, breeders bred dogs with different morphologies, or body types. Large, powerful dogs were required to guard livestock and homesteads, so the biggest dogs were selected for breeding. Conversely, to produce companion dogs, the smallest and cutest dogs were selected. Recently,

the advent of dog shows and the rise in the number of dogs kept solely as pets have resulted in dogs being selected for appearance only. Most breeders now produce dogs to win prizes at shows. The winners are the dogs that most closely resemble the breed standard – an arbitrary list of characteristics chosen by a committee of breeders.

◁ **Predation sequence**
The full behavioural pattern of a hunting wolf enables it to catch and kill the prey it needs to survive. These behaviours have been accentuated in different breeds to produce working dogs for varying purposes.

Catching   **Killing**   **Consuming**

Breed groupings

By tracing the history of breeds back to their beginnings, it is possible to find out what tasks the dogs were originally developed to perform. This allows us to categorize dog breeds according to their intended purpose.

The dogs in each of the categories below share common behaviour traits, for which they were bred selectively to make them good at their jobs. When kept as pets, they will all show similarities in the way they adapt to domestic life, and the problems that they encounter are likely to be the same. This helps us choose which dog is best suited to our lifestyle. As breeding becomes more selective, gene pools become smaller, and this results in a wide variety of inherited diseases in dog breeds. Always check carefully health certificates and bloodlines when purchasing a puppy, to ensure good health for the life of your dog.

Dogs to help hunters

These dogs were bred to help hunters shooting game in the field. They typically enjoy retrieving, and are usually very willing to please. They make very good pets, but their large size and high energy levels mean that they are not suitable for owners who do not have the same desire to exercise.

Golden Retriever

Dogs to help shepherds

Shepherd dogs fall into two groups: the popular herders and the less-well-known flock guardians. Herding dogs have high energy levels and a powerful desire to chase. Those bred to herd cattle usually have a stronger will than sheepdogs, but both enjoy a close bond with their owners. Flock guardians were bred to live with sheep, and are close-bonding and protective.

Border Collie

Dogs to hunt

Hunting dogs fall into two categories: those that hunt by sight, and those that follow trails. While good natured and easy going, they are independent and less willing to please than other dogs. They can cause problems on walks, as their desire to hunt is still very strong.

Beagle

Dogs to kill vermin

Bred to catch and kill, these tenacious, feisty breeds are popular as pets due to their small size, but owners should be aware of their propensity to be predatory towards small animals. They lean towards using aggression to solve problems, and need good early socialization and training. These dogs have strong personalities, and are great characters.

Jack Russell Terrier

Companion dogs

For generations, companion dogs have been bred as pets. They are sweet-natured and gentle, and their small size makes them easy to care for. Only a few of the breeds often classed as companion dogs were developed purely for this purpose; most were originally bred as watchdogs, or for some other type of work.

Chihuahua

Other working dogs

Many dogs were bred for other purposes, such as to guard, pull sleds, or fight. Each breed has a temperament to suit the work it was required to do; always investigate a breed's origins before buying, to see if it will make a suitable pet.

St Bernard

Carriage dogs
Dalmatians were bred to run alongside or under carriages, and to make a fashion statement. Since the breed was developed specifically for such a purpose, it is easy to train the dogs to behave like this for demonstrations.

Small dogs

Most small dogs tend to be easier to care for and keep clean, are cheaper to feed, and usually need less exercise than larger members of the species. Although they may be small, they usually have big personalities.

Small dogs are ideal for people who live in small spaces or urban areas, or who do not have the time to exercise a dog for several hours a day. They still need exercise and stimulation, but are usually content

◁ **Dachshund roll over**
Submission is a useful strategy for dealing with larger, assertive dogs as long as the bigger dog poses no real threat.

to receive less than their larger canine cousins. These little dogs often do not think of themselves as small, however, which makes them great as pets, but can also get them into trouble with bigger dogs. The temptation is for owners to protect them by keeping them away from large dogs who may harm them, but, if they are properly socialized, small dogs can hold their

◁ **Sweet but spirited**
A large dog in a small body, this West Highland Terrier looks sweet, but has a strong character.

own, and many develop effective strategies for dealing with larger dogs. It can be tempting to treat small dogs as toys, but owners must be careful to ensure that all of their dog's needs are met, and they are given every opportunity to indulge in natural canine behaviour.

Chihuahua

Size	1–3kg (2–6lb), 16–22cm (6–9in)
Character	Feisty, lively, loyal
Exercise	Minimal
Grooming	Minimal

 This active little dog originated in Mexico as early as the 9th century. The Chihuahua's most likely ancestor is a dog called the Techchi, from the Toltec civilization. The introduction of hairless Oriental genes has made the modern Chihuahua smaller than its predecessor— Chihuahuas are the smallest of all dogs, and come in both long-haired and short-haired varieties. Due to their diminutive size, Chihuahuas are easily damaged, making them unsuitable for clumsy adults or families with toddlers. They need good early socialization and protection from being overwhelmed when living in a world of giants.

Large, erect ears

Short-haired Chihuahua

Fringed tail

Long-haired Chihuahua

Maltese

Size	1–3kg (2–6lb), 16–22cm (6–9in)
Character	Friendly, fun-loving, playful
Exercise	Minimal
Grooming	Daily grooming and regular clipping

Originally an ancient breed from the island of Malta, these small dogs have been bred as companions for many generations. The result is a happy little dog, who makes an ideal pet for those owners who enjoy caring for his long coat. Maltese dogs require regular visits to the grooming salon, and the hair on their head must be clipped or tied to enable them to see out.

Yorkshire Terrier

Size *1–3kg (2–6lb), 16–22cm (6–9in)*
Character *Lively, feisty, courageous*
Exercise *Minimal to moderate*
Grooming *Daily grooming and regular clipping*

This dog originated in Yorkshire in the 19th century, where it was bred by coal miners and mill workers to kill rats. It is very much a terrier, and many Yorkshire Terrier owners are taken by surprise when their small companions unveil their feisty nature if they are threatened. Yorkshire Terriers need plenty of early socialization to make them feel content and at peace with the world around them, and also to prevent them becoming too protective of their owners. They are active, intelligent, and playful, and will readily learn any exercise you wish to teach them. A Yorkshire Terrier's coat does not shed, and requires daily grooming to stay in good condition. The hair around their eyes needs to be clipped or tied up to enable them to see where they are going.

△ **Energetic dogs**
Although small, Yorkshire Terriers are very active. They need the freedom to run and play, especially when young.

Toy Poodle

Size *1–3kg (2–6lb), 16–22cm (6–9in)*
Character *Intelligent, good natured, lively*
Exercise *Moderate*
Grooming *Daily grooming and regular clipping*

The smallest of all the poodles, the Toy was bred from the Standard Poodle, whose original function was as a duck retriever. This graceful, athletic little dog is clever, easy to train, and benefits from a lively household with plenty of stimulation. Coat care is an important consideration for prospective owners.

Pomeranian

Size *1–3kg (2–6lb), 16–22cm (6–9in)*
Character *Active, intelligent, good watchdog*
Exercise *Minimal to moderate*
Grooming *Daily, extensive grooming*

Pomeranians originated in Poland and Germany, from spitz-type Arctic sled dogs. Miniaturized by selective breeding, they retain the extrovert character of their ancestors, and excessive barking can be a problem. Their thick coat can make them excessively hot in warm climates.

Miniature Pinscher

Size *1–3kg (2–6lb), 16–22cm (6–9in)*
Character *Active, protective, clever*
Exercise *Moderate*
Grooming *Minimal*

The Miniature Pinscher was bred in the 19th century, to kill rats on German farms. Small and feisty, this little dog has a terrier's hunting instincts. Miniature Pinschers need good socialization as puppies and plenty of attention and stimulation in their home.

Tan and black coat

Bichon Frise

Size *1–3kg (2–6lb), 16–22cm (6–9in)*
Character *Playful, good-natured, sociable*
Exercise *Minimal to moderate*
Grooming *Daily grooming and regular clipping*

The exact origins of the Bichon Frise are unclear, but bichon-type dogs have been traced back thousands of years. Popular for many centuries in France and Spain, the Bichon Frise was developed on the island of Tenerife. Its characteristic friendly temperament and its happy disposition come from a long history of being bred as a companion. This agile little dog is sweet-natured and lovable.

Havanese

Size *1–3kg (2–6lb), 16–22cm (6–9in)*
Character *Playful, good-natured, sociable*
Exercise *Minimal to moderate*
Grooming *Daily grooming*

In the 16th century, bichon-type dogs travelled with Spanish sailors to Cuba, where they developed into today's Havanese and became the Cuban national dog. With a lighter weight and more silky coat than the Bichon Frise, these dogs are better suited to a warmer climate and were bred for centuries as companions. As a result, they have a happy, friendly temperament, making them ideal pets. They benefit from having the hair on their head clipped or tied up to enable them to see out.

Long, soft double coat

Plumed tail

Miniature Poodle

Size *1–3kg (2–6lb), 16–22cm (6–9in)*
Character *Intelligent, agile, good-natured*
Exercise *Moderate*
Grooming *Daily grooming and regular clipping*

The name Poodle comes from the German word *pudel*, which means to splash in water – the ancestors of the modern Poodle were bred in the 15th century to hunt water birds. Later, the French developed the Poodle into three sizes, the Miniature being the middle size. Miniature Poodles are clever and agile and made good circus performers. Nowadays, they are commonly owned by agility and obedience competitors, and they make very energetic, smart workers. The Poodle's pom-poms were once thought necessary to protect the working dogs' joints from cold water, but most pet poodles now have a simple clip, trimmed to the same length all over.

Dense, curly coat

Small, compact feet

Boston Terrier

Size *1–3kg (2–6lb), 16–22cm (6–9in)*
Character *Gentle, good-natured, enthusiastic*
Exercise *Minimal to moderate*
Grooming *Minimal*

Bred in Boston, Massachusetts, USA, in the mid-19th century from bulldogs, terriers, and French Bulldogs, the Boston Terrier has retained very little of its true terrier nature. These dogs are sweet-natured and sociable, but their shortened nose can lead to snoring, as well as breathing problems during exercise.

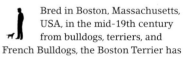

Papillon

Size *1–3kg (2–6lb), 16–22cm (6–9in)*
Character *Intelligent, lively, sensitive*
Exercise *Moderate*
Grooming *Daily grooming*

The Papillon's ancestors have been featured in paintings since the 16th century. The name Papillon, or "butterfly dog", is taken from the way its large, long-haired ears resemble a butterfly's wings when held erect. These are energetic little dogs and, although dainty, they are robust and active. They are intelligent and easily learn what is required.

Shih Tzu

Size *1–3kg (2–6lb), 16–22cm (6–9in)*
Character *Intelligent, independent, alert*
Exercise *Moderate*
Grooming *Daily grooming; occasional clipping*

Bred by Tibetan monks and Chinese Emperors, the Shih Tzu is named after the lion it was thought to resemble. Without correct socializing, these intelligent, alert little dogs can be bad tempered. The hair on their head needs to be clipped or tied up, and their shortened faces can lead to breathing difficulties.

Parson Russell Terrier

Size *1–3kg (2–6lb), 16–22cm (6–9in)*
Character *Feisty, active, tenacious*
Exercise *High*
Grooming *Minimal*

The Parson Russell Terrier was created in the 19th century to run with hounds and flush foxes from their lairs. Less common than the shorter-legged Jack Russell, the Parson is recognized by Kennel Clubs and holds a true pedigree. Like most terriers, they are quite predatory, and need socializing with cats from an early age. Most cannot be trusted around small pets. They are friendly and outgoing if socialized well with people and other dogs, but can be difficult and confrontational if this is not done adequately. Parson Russell Terriers are intelligent and active, and they suit a home where there is always plenty of activity.

Broad skull

Muscular hind legs

Jack Russell Terrier

The shorter-legged Jack Russell Terrier is not recognized by Kennel Clubs. This dog comes in many forms and varieties, and it benefits health-wise from a larger gene pool. In temperament and character, it is very similar to its taller cousins and needs careful socialization and education.

Border Terrier

Size *1–3kg (2–6lb), 16–22cm (6–9in)*
Character *Friendly, active, biddable*
Exercise *Moderate*
Grooming *Minimal plus periodic stripping*

Border Terriers were bred in Scotland in the 18th century, to kill foxes and rodents. Their small size and happy attitude make them popular pets. Although they need careful socialization with cats and other dogs, they are easily controlled. Fun-loving and easy to live with, Border Terriers readily adapt their exercise levels to those of their owners. They are bright little dogs who love human company, although they are also independent enough to be left alone. Border Terriers do well at agility, being fast and supple. Naturally curious, they make very pleasant companions if they are well socialized and educated.

Stiff outer coat

Darkish, dropped ears

Tail thicker at base

Straight forelegs

△ **Active pets**
Border Terriers are happy to go out for long walks but also happy to sit on your lap.

Cavalier King Charles

Size *1–3kg (2–6lb), 16–22cm (6–9in)*
Character *Friendly, sweet-natured, playful*
Exercise *Moderate*
Grooming *Daily grooming*

With a less flattened face than the King Charles Spaniel, which is a different breed, the Cavalier King Charles has a longer nose, as well as a flatter skull. Sadly, inherited diseases abound within the small gene pool for this breed. Cavaliers are true pets, having been bred for centuries to be companions, and make lovely family dogs if you can find a healthy one.

Long, silky coat

Lhasa Apso

Size *1–3kg (2–6lb), 16–22cm (6–9in)*
Character *Alert, active, vocal*
Exercise *Moderate*
Grooming *Extensive daily grooming*

Bred by monks in Tibetan temples and monasteries to be watchdogs, these dogs will let you know when they detect intruders. Strong-willed and intelligent, they need good training and education. Lhasa Apsos have a thick coat designed to keep them warm in a cold climate, so require extensive grooming.

Fairly narrow skull

Dense, straight coat

Tail carried over back

Cairn Terrier

Size *1–3kg (2–6lb), 16–22cm (6–9in)*
Character *Active, playful, sociable*
Exercise *Moderate*
Grooming *Minimal plus periodic stripping*

A working terrier from as far back as the 17th century, this playful dog originated from the Scottish Highlands and islands. Bred to hunt foxes, rats, and rabbits around the cairns (rock piles), it still retains some of its predatory nature, and care is needed when it is around small pets. Early socialization with cats is also advisable. Lively and sociable, Cairn Terriers need to be kept busy.

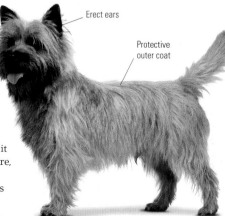

Erect ears

Protective outer coat

Miniature Schnauzer

Size *1–3kg (2–6lb), 16–22cm (6–9 in)*
Character *Lively, playful, sociable*
Exercise *Moderate*
Grooming *Daily grooming plus regular clipping*

This dog was developed in Germany in the 19th century from the Standard Schnauzer. Used as a watchdog and controller of vermin on farms, the modern-day breed still has a predatory streak, and likes to warn its owners of intruders. Miniature Schnauzers are intelligent and playful and make good family pets.

Thick, wiry coat

Long beard

Pug

Size *1–3kg (2–6lb), 16–22cm (6–9in)*
Character *Friendly, outgoing, good-natured*
Exercise *Minimal*
Grooming *Minimal*

Possibly bred originally by the Chinese, pug-like dogs rapidly spread throughout Europe in the 16th century. Modern-day Pugs have a small gene pool, which leads to inherited health problems, including some breathing difficulties and snoring. They are popular despite this, because of their excellent temperament.

West Highland Terrier

Size *1–3kg (2–6lb), 16–22cm (6–9in)*
Character *Feisty, active, vocal*
Exercise *Moderate*
Grooming *Daily brushing and regular clipping*

West Highland Terriers were developed in the 18th century from the white offspring of Cairn and Scottish Terriers. They were bred to hunt small prey, so be wary around small pets and cats. Take care to find a healthy dog as skin complaints are a common problem. They make very good pets for strong-willed owners.

Dachshund

Size *1–3kg (2–6lb), 16–22cm (6–9in)*
Character *Placid, playful, easy-going*
Exercise *Moderate*
Grooming *Minimal*

Dachshunds were originally developed in Germany in the 20th century to hunt badgers. They come in two sizes – miniature and standard – and in three coat types. Dachshunds frequently suffer from bad backs because of their long spines and short ribcages, and slipped discs are common. Care should be taken when lifting these dogs, and children should be discouraged from rough play. Happy, laid-back personalities make Dachshunds gentle companions.

A varied coat
Dachshunds come in three different coat types. The long-haired variety requires more extensive grooming than the other two.

Smooth-haired Dachshund

Wire-haired Dachshund

Prominent eye ridges

Silky ears

Long-haired Dachshund

Medium dogs

Medium-sized dogs are less of a handful than the larger breeds, but have more of a presence than smaller dogs. They are big enough not to be easily trampled, yet not too big for small spaces.

For people who do not have room for a large dog but feel they need something more substantial than a small breed, a medium-sized dog is ideal. These dogs are at home in

most moderately-sized houses. Medium-sized dogs are usually robust enough to play with children, and are not easily damaged by play or other activities. While they require less feeding than larger dogs, their exercise needs vary – certain breeds actually require more activity than some of their bigger cousins. Compared to large dogs, medium-sized dogs are easier

◁ **Just right**
More substantial than a small dog but less work than a large breed, medium dogs, like this French Bulldog, can be ideal companions.

to handle when excited, and less likely to pull you over. Their compact size also reduces household cleaning, and there is less chance of their wagging tails knocking things over. Health insurance is usually less expensive than for larger breeds.

▷ **Good family pets**
Less fragile than small dogs, medium-sized dogs, such as this Fox Terrier, can be perfect pets for active owners.

Shetland Sheepdog

Size 6–7kg (13–15lb), 35–37cm (14–15in)
Character Timid, gentle, sensitive
Exercise Moderate
Grooming Extensive daily grooming

Shetland Sheepdogs were developed in the 17th century, to herd livestock in the Shetland Islands of Scotland. They were originally a cross of the larger Rough Collie with smaller breeds. Modern Shetland Sheepdogs have a thick coat that can cause overheating. They need early, thorough socialization to counteract their natural wariness. These playful and sweet-natured dogs will be very loyal to trusted owners.

French Bulldog

Size 10–12.5kg (22–28lb), 30–31cm (12in)
Character Affectionate, outgoing, good-natured
Exercise Minimal
Grooming Minimal

The origins of French Bulldogs are unclear, but they are likely to have been the smaller progeny of English Bulldogs taken over to France in the 19th century. French Bulldogs have been bred as companions for generations and, as a result, they are good tempered, fun-loving extroverts. Their flattened faces can cause breathing difficulties and also snoring.

Tibetan Terrier

Size 8–13.5kg (18–30lb), 36–41cm (14–16in)
Character Intelligent, vocal, enthusiastic
Exercise Moderate
Grooming Needs daily grooming and regular clipping

Tibetan Terriers were bred as watchdogs by monks in Tibet and are probably the ancestors of similar breeds such as the Shih Tzu and Lhasa Apso. These dogs are lively and vivacious, but need careful socialization and early training to be well behaved. Tibetan Terriers are also very vocal, as might be expected from their heritage, and this needs to be kept within boundaries.

Corgi

Size *11–17kg (24–37lb), 27–32cm (11–13in)*
Character *Intelligent, protective, loyal*
Exercise *Moderate*
Grooming *Minimal*

Of the two Corgi breeds, the Cardigan and the Pembroke Welsh, the latter is more common due to its connection with the British Royal Family. Both breeds were developed in Wales to herd livestock. This required a strong will, and owners need to be prepared to win challenges and set guidelines. Good socialization will overcome the dogs' natural reserve, and ensure that defensive nipping at heels does not become a problem. Corgis are playful and active, and benefit from lively owners.

Cardigan Corgi

Pembroke Welsh Corgi

Staffordshire Bull Terrier

Size *11–17kg (24–37lb), 36–41cm (14–16in)*
Character *Enthusiastic, playful, energetic*
Exercise *High*
Grooming *Minimal*

Staffordshire Bull Terriers were bred in England in the early 19th century for fighting other dogs in pits after bull and bear baiting were outlawed. They were bred to be determined and courageous – traits that they retain today. Early and careful socialization with other dogs is needed to ensure they remain friendly. Being playful and eager, they make excellent companions for children. Staffordshire Bull Terriers need an active family that can channel the dogs' excess energy into constructive play with toys.

Fox Terrier

Size *7–8kg (15–18lb), 39–40cm (15–16in)*
Character *Feisty, lively, impulsive*
Exercise *Moderate to high*
Grooming *Minimal*

The two Fox Terrier breeds, the Smooth and the Wire, share the same origins: they were developed to unearth foxes gone to ground during hunting. They also display similar characteristics because they did not become two distinct breeds until the early 20th century. These clever, affectionate dogs are agile, active, and playful, with high levels of energy. They are easily aroused and ready for a scrap, should they feel one is needed. Fox Terriers make good pets for owners capable of handling their strong terrier nature and their predatory instincts.

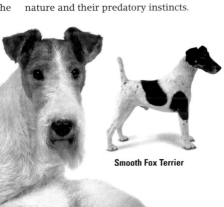

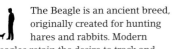

Smooth Fox Terrier

Wire Fox Terrier

Beagle

Size *8–14kg (18–31lb), 33–40cm (13–16in)*
Character *Sociable, independent, vocal*
Exercise *Moderate to high*
Grooming *Minimal*

The Beagle is an ancient breed, originally created for hunting hares and rabbits. Modern Beagles retain the desire to track and hunt, which may cause control problems on walks. Beagles have a happy disposition, and readily get on with others – human or animal.

Whippet

Size *12.5–13.5kg (28–30lb), 43–50cm (17–20in)*
Character *Gentle, calm, affectionate*
Exercise *Moderate*
Grooming *Moderate*

Whippets were created in the mid-19th century from Greyhounds and terriers, for hunting rabbits and small game. These sight hounds have a strong desire to chase. This tendency, combined with their fast speed, makes them difficult to control on walks. At home they are calm and affectionate. Whippets need protection in cold weather because of their thin coats.

Long, lean muzzle

Muscular hind legs

Brittany

Size *13–15kg (29–33lb), 47–50cm (19–20in)*
Character *Intelligent, active, keen*
Exercise *High*
Grooming *High*

Developed in the Brittany region of northwest France in the 19th century, this breed was formed from a mixture of English Setters and Pointers, together with local spaniels. The smallest of the hunt-point-retrieve breeds, it was originally used to aid hunters on rough shoots. Brittanys are clever and quick to learn, and need owners who are able to channel their considerable energy into useful work. They are very affectionate and biddable, and are happy to work at any task required. Brittanys make good companions for lively families.

Fine, dense coat

High-set ears, rounded at tip

Cocker Spaniel

Size *13–15kg (29–33lb), 38–41cm (15–16in)*
Character *Biddable, active, affectionate*
Exercise *High*
Grooming *Regular brushing, especially the ears*

There are two breeds of Cocker Spaniel, English and American (not shown). Cocker Spaniels were originally bred in England to hunt woodcock, being small enough to flush the birds from their hiding places. English Cockers went to America with the early settlers, where the breed was developed into the American Cocker. These dogs can be willful, so owners need to set boundaries for good behaviour early on. Relatively small in size and with a happy disposition, the Cocker Spaniel has been one of the most popular breeds for many years.

◁ **Ready to go**
Cocker Spaniels are full of life. They need owners who can give them the opportunity to use up their considerable energy as well as providing training and leadership.

Long, silky ears

Soft, medium-length coat

Feathered chest

English Cocker Spaniel

Springer Spaniel

Size *22–24kg (49–53lb), 48–51cm (19–20in)*

Character *Energetic, playful, enthusiastic*

Exercise *Very high*

Grooming *Moderate*

Springer Spaniels were developed from Spanish Spaniels in the 19th century to flush out or "spring" gamebirds, and return them to the handler once shot. They are friendly and sociable, and it is unusual to find one with a bad temperament. Springers are easily trained, taking direction readily and accepting whatever role they are given. While they may seem like the perfect dog, their energy levels are higher than many people can cope with. Owners need time for long walks and games. They do best in a busy home where there is lots of excitement and interest for them.

▷ **Willing worker**
Springers are tireless and always ready for more. They make good pets for busy, active families who have time for long walks, lots of games, and fun.

Silky coat

Feathering on legs

Shar Pei

Size *16–20kg (35–44lb), 46–51cm (18–20in)*

Character *Aloof, reserved, loyal*

Exercise *Moderate*

Grooming *Time is needed to care for deep skin folds*

Originating from China and sharing a common ancestor with the Chow Chow, the Shar Pei was bred for a variety of uses, including guarding, herding, and hunting. The fashion to exaggerate the wrinkles makes for appealing puppies, but it can result in infected skin folds and cause eyelashes to turn in against the eye – a painful condition requiring surgery. Shar Peis need good socialization as puppies.

Exaggerated skin folds

Bulldog

Size *23–25kg (51–55lb), 30–36cm (12–14in)*

Character *Sociable, courageous, loyal*

Exercise *Minimal*

Grooming *Minimal*

Bulldogs were bred in the 17th century for bull- and bear-baiting. When these sports were outlawed, pug genes were introduced to produce a shorter, squarer dog with a squashed face. These features have been exaggerated over the years. As a result, breathing is compromised in Bulldogs and they suffer heat stress, snore, and cannot exercise much. The wide head means that they are unable to be born naturally. Known for their friendliness, these natural clowns show great affection towards their owners.

Bull Terrier

Size *24–28kg (53–62lb), 53–56cm (21–22in)*

Character *Feisty, persistent, loyal*

Exercise *Moderate to high*

Grooming *Minimal*

Bull Terriers were created in the 19th century, when Bulldogs were crossed with English White Terriers to produce a white "Gentleman's Companion". Modern Bull Terriers come in a variety of colours. Bull terriers are energetic but prefer to play rather than run. Tug games are their favourites, and owners need to be careful to remain in control. Bull terriers suit busy, active families who can give them plenty of stimulation.

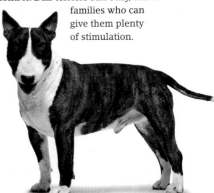

Large dogs

Owners of large dogs need lots of spare time and energy for exercising, playing, grooming, and general maintenance. Plenty of room is needed, both inside the house and outside, as well as areas for long walks off-lead.

Larger breeds usually make far more demanding pets than smaller dogs. They not only require you to devote more time and energy to them, but they are also likely to result in considerably higher bills.

◁ **Low but large**
The Basset Hound is a big dog with short legs. Holding on to a Basset Hound that wants to run takes a lot of strength, so these dogs need to be taught not to pull from a very early age.

That said, there are many benefits from keeping a big dog, and many people opt for a larger breed.

Unlike small breeds, large dogs won't get under your feet without you seeing them. They also offer a powerful deterrent to burglars and muggers, and they can help your children to feel safer. Many large dogs are easier to train than their smaller cousins, and a well-trained large dog looks very impressive. They are often faster and more energetic than small dogs – traits that are appreciated by owners who

enjoy dog sports such as agility, or have other active pursuits in which their dog can participate.

△ **Born to run**
Dalmatians were bred to run. They need to be taught a good recall as puppies, and have safe areas where they can run freely as adults.

Border Collie

Height	14–22kg (31–49lb), 46–54cm (18–21in)
Character	Intelligent, reactive, close-bonding
Exercise	Very high
Grooming	Moderate

Border Collies were bred in the early 20th century for sheepdog work on the English and Scottish borders. A good demonstration of sheep herding often convinces people that these dogs have an innate capacity to understand humans; in reality, they need training just like other dogs. However, Border Collies are quick to learn and willing to take instruction, and they establish close bonds with their owners. Lots of early socialization will ensure that their reactivity does not lead to noise phobias or fear-related problems.

Herding

Border Collies are still popular as sheepdogs and excess working dogs often find their way into pet homes. Selective breeding has enhanced their desire to chase, and they will quickly learn to herd and chase whatever moves around them. If they are to be kept as a pet, these instincts need to be channelled into games with toys to prevent them from chasing after joggers, cats, livestock, and cars.

Siberian Husky

Size *16–27.5kg (35–60lb), 51–60cm (20–24in)*
Character *Active, intelligent, independent*
Exercise *Very high*
Grooming *Extensive daily grooming needed*

Siberian Huskies were once essential to the Chuckchi people of Siberia, whose culture was based around being able to travel long distances by dog-sled. These dogs have the stamina to run all day, and they need considerable daily exercise. As a result, this is a breed for serious enthusiasts who can run the dogs across country in carts or on bikes. The predatory nature of Siberians means that they cannot be let off-lead near livestock and other animals. A lively, active home is a must for Siberians.

Thick, bushy tail

Muscular thighs

Tough, cushioned pads

Strong, deep chest

Basset Hound

Size *18–27kg (40–60lb), 33–38cm (13–15in)*
Character *Sweet-natured, sociable, independent*
Exercise *High*
Grooming *Minimal*

Basset Hounds were bred for hunting rabbits by scent. They are easily distracted by animal trails, and may be difficult to recall from a scent. While this causes control problems on walks, they are popular pets due to their happy disposition and sociable nature.

Long, low-set ears

Bearded Collie

Height *18–30kg (40–66lb), 50–56cm (20–22in)*
Character *Playful, active, sensitive*
Exercise *Very high*
Grooming *Extensive daily grooming needed*

Bred in the 16th century from a mixture of the Polish Lowland Sheepdogs and local Collies in Scotland, Bearded Collies were used for sheep and cattle herding. Modern Bearded Collies retain a strong desire to chase and herd, so owners need to channel the abundant energy of these fun-loving dogs into play-chases with toys. They are sensitive and need good early socialization.

Long, dense, fine coat

Australian Shepherd

Height *16–32kg (35–70lb), 46–58cm (18–23in)*
Character *Intelligent, strong-willed, active*
Exercise *Very high*
Grooming *Moderate*

Almost unknown in Australia, the Australian Shepherd Dog was developed on ranches in the western USA in the 19th and 20th centuries from a variety of sheepdogs. These dogs have a strong work ethic and need plenty of stimulation and activity. They also need owners with a will strong enough to match their own.

Weather-resistant, medium-length coat

Rough Collie

Height *18–30kg (40–66lb), 50–60cm (20–24in)*
Character *Sensitive, loyal, gentle*
Exercise *Moderate*
Grooming *Extensive daily grooming*

Rough Collies were bred to herd sheep in Scotland. Although still interested in chasing and play, today's Rough Collies are intelligent and learn quickly. Careful socialization is needed to develop a relaxed adult, as their timid nature readily leads to fears. Rough Collies thrive in quiet homes with gentle, relaxed, thoughtful owners.

Abundant, smooth, shiny coat

Forelegs are well feathered

Standard Poodle

Size *20.5–32kg (45–70lb), over 38cm (15in)*
Character *Intelligent, good-natured, active*
Exercise *High to very high*
Grooming *Needs daily grooming and regular clipping*

First bred in Germany in the 15th century to help on duck hunts, and later developed by the French, this is the largest of the Poodles. The curly coat, which kept the dog warm in cold water during retrieves, does not shed and needs a lot of care. Quick to learn, affectionate, and playful, Standards benefit from active owners.

Long hair covering ears

Straight, parallel forelegs

Airedale Terrier

Size *20–22.5kg (44–50lb), 56–61cm (22–24in)*
Character *Intelligent, courageous, loyal*
Exercise *Moderate*
Grooming *Requires periodic stripping of dead coat*

Airedales were developed in the 19th century in Yorkshire, England, to hunt otters and badgers, and also to act as guard dogs. Modern day Airedale Terriers are protective and need plenty of socialization to be friendly, especially around other dogs. They are playful and good with children. Best suited to owners who have experience and a strong character, Airedales are not easy to train or to handle when in difficult situations. Since they have the hunting instincts of a terrier, they should not be trusted with unfamiliar cats or other small pets.

△ **Steady nature**
Airedales are loyal to owners and make good family dogs if they are well trained and socialized as puppies.

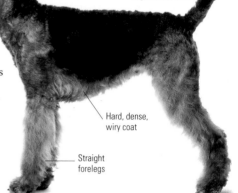

High-set tail

Hard, dense, wiry coat

Straight forelegs

German Short-haired Pointer

Size *20–30kg (44–66lb), 60–65cm (24–26in)*
Character *Sociable, energetic, playful*
Exercise *Very high*
Grooming *Minimal*

German Short-haired Pointers were created in Germany in the 19th century from Spanish and English Pointers, mixed with Foxhounds and other good scenting dogs. These excellent, all-purpose gun dogs are capable of hunting, pointing, and retrieving. The German Short-haired Pointer is agile and active, with plenty of stamina, and owners need to provide plenty of stimulation and exercise. Fortunately, being naturally playful, its boundless energy is easily diverted into games with toys. These dogs are good-natured, willing to please, and easy to train.

Dalmatian

Size *22.5–25kg (50–55lb), 50–61cm (20–24in)*
Character *Independent, outgoing, sociable*
Exercise *Very high*
Grooming *Minimal*

This ancient breed is thought to have originated in Dalmatia, Croatia. Bred to run with carriages in England and with fire engines in the USA, it is a natural athlete, and may become boisterous if denied the opportunity to exercise. Dalmatians are generally easy-going, but may sometimes be willful and obstinate.

Short, glossy, and spotted coat

Tail curves upwards slightly

Compact feet

Boxer

Size	*25–32kg (55–70lb), 53–63cm (21–25in)*
Character	*Exuberant, playful, friendly*
Exercise	*Very high*
Grooming	*Minimal*

Boxers were developed in Germany from the English Bulldog and the Bullenbeisser, a now-extinct breed used to hunt bears, wild boar, and deer. They were bred to chase and seize prey, holding on until hunters arrived. Not surprisingly, the modern descendants of these dogs are courageous and strong-minded enough to take on opponents if necessary.

Usually, however, Boxers are loveable clowns. The name Boxer comes from their tendency to "box" with their front paws during play, which they may find easier than play-biting due to their flattened faces and undershot bites. Boxers make great family dogs, being playful and fun-loving with children, and are a consistently popular dog around the world for this reason. They need plenty to do, and are best-suited to active families who want to include their dog in all aspects of their busy lives.

Early socialization is essential for Boxers, especially with other dogs, to

Children's playmate

The Boxer's readiness to play makes it an excellent companion for children, who help to use up its considerable energy reserves and provide the lively, high-spirited interaction that really suits this breed. As with all dogs, rules for games must be taught to both parties to avoid play getting out of hand.

ensure that they grow up friendly. Also essential are consistent guidelines for good behaviour, implemented early in life so that their exuberance and strong character are kept within bounds. Strong-willed owners who use positive training methods will get the best out of this engaging breed.

Boxers are intelligent and relatively easy to train, but they can be cheeky and prone to disobedience if rules for good behaviour are not firmly established.

Because of their flattened face and undershot jaw – characteristics selected for in order to give them a strong biting grip – Boxers can be prone to dribbling and snoring.

Undershot jaw

Short, shiny, smooth hair covering extensive deep chest

Strong, straight forelegs

△ **On guard**
Boxers can be distrustful of strangers, and are easily aroused by intruders. This characteristic can be useful when there is a real threat to the safety of the family. However, careful training is needed to ensure that this trait does not get out of hand and result in unwanted aggression.

Labrador Retriever

Size	*25–36kg (55–79lb), 55–62cm (22–24in)*
Character	*Biddable, sociable, playful*
Exercise	*Very high*
Grooming	*Minimal*

Labradors originated on the island of Newfoundland, Canada, in the 15th century, where they were used by fishermen to retrieve and pull in nets from the water. In the 19th century, they were taken to England and developed as gun dogs to assist with duck shooting.

Labradors are one of the most popular breeds, being versatile, well-balanced, and easy to train. Often kept as pets or gun dogs, their good temperament and biddability has also made them the breed of choice for assistance dogs, helping people with disabilities to perform everyday tasks more easily, and giving them independence. The powerful scent-detecting abilities of Labradors have made them useful in the fight against drugs, and they also help to stop food, narcotics, and explosives from getting through customs. Finding bodies, alive or dead, is another invaluable task they are trained to perform by firefighters and police officers.

As pets, Labradors are playful and energetic. They do best in homes where there is lots of activity and plenty to do. They adore food, and stealing from the bin or kitchen work surfaces will need to be prevented and discouraged from the outset. Weight control is also important, as this is a breed that will eat far more than it needs, especially when neutered.

Labradors need careful training when young to make sure that their natural enthusiasm does not get them into trouble. Fortunately, this is easily done, since they are always willing to please and very amenable to doing as you ask.

△ **Playful character**
A pet Labrador's enthusiasm and energy need to be channelled into games with toys to prevent unacceptable behaviour. Their love of retrieving will mean that they get tired long before you do.

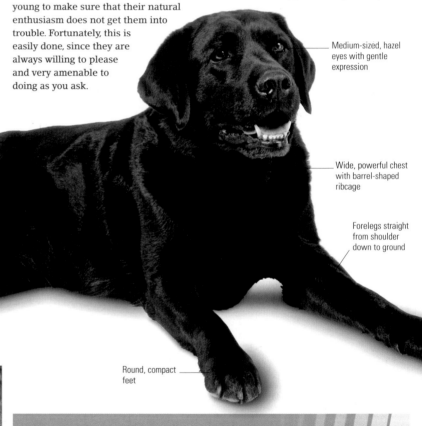

Medium-sized, hazel eyes with gentle expression

Wide, powerful chest with barrel-shaped ribcage

Forelegs straight from shoulder down to ground

Thick tail is otter-like in shape

Round, compact feet

△ **Plenty of energy**
Labradors need lots of off-lead running to keep them fit. Training a recall allows you to let them run freely and safely. Early socialization with other dogs and careful training with other animals and livestock will create a dog that is a joy to take out.

Guide dogs

Purpose-bred to be steady, careful workers, guide dogs are trusted with guiding blind people around obstacles and waiting at roadsides until it is safe to cross. Training takes several years but, once complete, the guide dogs give their handlers a new-found independence and freedom.

Hovawart

Size *25–41kg (55–90lb), 58–70cm (23–28in)*

Character *Intelligent, loyal, protective*

Exercise *Very high*

Grooming *Moderate*

Hovawart means "Guardian of Property" in German, which gives a clue to the origins of these clever dogs. As well as guarding, this ancient breed was used to herd and help with livestock. Hovawarts are good at protecting the family from intruders, but careful socialization and training is needed to ensure that they are tolerant of strangers. Hovawarts learn readily, and are loving and loyal to their owners.

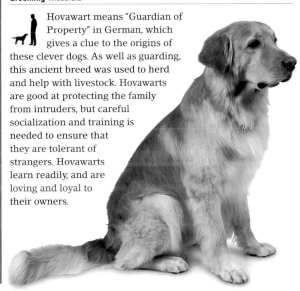

German Wire-haired Pointer

Height *27–32kg (60–70lb), 61–68cm (24–27in)*

Character *Biddable, energetic, playful*

Exercise *Very high*

Grooming *Minimal*

Bred in Germany from the German Pointer and a variety of other breeds, the Wire-haired Pointer was developed as a versatile, rugged gun dog. More wary of strangers than their short-haired cousins, they need careful early socialization. That said, they are affectionate towards their owners, willing to please, and able to learn tasks with ease.

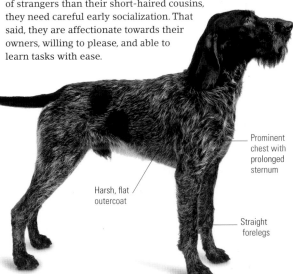

Prominent chest with prolonged sternum

Harsh, flat outercoat

Straight forelegs

Belgian Shepherd

Size *27.5–28.5kg (61–63lb), 56–66cm (22–26in)*

Character *Reactive, intelligent, protective*

Exercise *Very high*

Grooming *Depends on variety*

The different varieties of Belgian Shepherd are named after the areas from which they came. They are all of a similar type, and were bred to herd sheep and guard farms. These very sensitive dogs need lots of early socialization and habituation to humans, animals, and every day life. They are easy to train, loyal, and devoted to their owners. Belgian Shepherds do well with thoughtful owners who are good leaders, and who can provide plenty of activity.

Deep chest

Forelegs held close to body

Malinois

Tervueren

Groenendael

The same breed?
In their home country of Belgium, these four varieties are considered one breed. Other countries have registered them as four separate breeds. In reality, they are so closely related that puppies with all four different types of coat can be found in the same litter.

High-set, stiff ears

Long, bushy tail

Laekenois

Golden Retriever

Size	27–36kg (60–79lb), 51–61cm (20–24in)
Character	Sociable, playful, kind
Exercise	High
Grooming	Daily grooming required

The Golden Retriever was first bred in the 19th century from a variety of sporting dogs to produce a robust, powerful gun dog with a gentle and biddable nature. Today, its good temperament is the dog's most important feature, which explains its enduring popularity as a family pet. Golden Retrievers are playful and energetic, but not so active that they require round-the-clock activity. Happy to sleep and rest at home, they have bags of energy outside and plenty of stamina to work or play all day. Owners of Golden Retrievers will need lots of time for dog-centred activities, games, and fun.

Being cheerful and obliging, Golden Retrievers make good companions for children, provided that the dogs are socialized with them from an early age and taught good manners.

Ever willing to undertake tasks and easy to train, Golden Retrievers make ideal working dogs. They are regularly used in detection and therapy work, and as assistance dogs such as guide dogs.

Bringing back

A well-bred Golden Retriever can easily be taught to fetch. Take care to obtain puppies from biddable parents, since some of show strains are too possessive. Early training and plenty of play will ensure that your dog returns the objects you throw, so that he does the running rather than you.

△ **Plenty of energy**
Golden Retrievers have boundless energy for running, walks, and dog sports. They suit busy homes where they can be included in all aspects of family life.

Ears set level with eyes

Dark-pigmented lips

Wavy coat; may also be flat

Strong hindquarters

Well-feathered tail

Flat-coated Retriever

Height	25–36kg (55–79lb), 56–61cm (22–24in)
Character	Gentle, affectionate, outgoing
Exercise	High
Grooming	Minimal

Originating in England in the mid-19th century, the Flat-coated Retriever was bred as a general-purpose gun dog. Its gentle, playful, attentive nature makes it an ideal family pet. Flat-coated Retrievers are eager to learn and always ready to retrieve. Their activity levels are high, and they need plenty to do to use up surplus energy, but they are not clumsy or over-boisterous. Flat-coated Retrievers are poor guard dogs, since they are happy to welcome anyone. This makes them ideal for novice and sociable owners. Willing and able to please, Flatcoats make happy workers and loving companions.

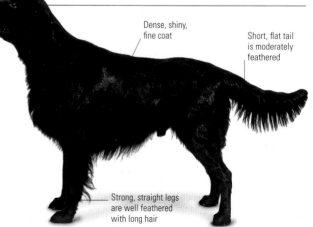

Dense, shiny, fine coat

Short, flat tail is moderately feathered

Strong, straight legs are well feathered with long hair

German Shepherd Dog

Size *28–44kg (62–97lb), 55–66cm (22–26in)*
Character *Intelligent, protective, loyal*
Exercise *Very high*
Grooming *Daily, especially for long-coated varieties*

This popular breed was created in Germany in the late 19th century to herd sheep and protect property. At the end of World War I, it became known as the Alsatian in the UK, the name change reflecting the anti-German feeling in the country at the time. Only 50 years later did the breed regain its correct name, and these dogs are sometimes still referred to as Alsatians by mistake.

German Shepherds are quick, clever learners, and their intelligence is highly valued by those who work them. As well as carrying out police-dog work, they often act as guards for the military and private security companies. They are also used for search-and-rescue work, and in scent-detection roles to locate hidden narcotics, explosives, and even human remains.

German Shepherds make good pets for owners who like to train and play, and they are good with children. Extremely loyal, they will protect both family and property from any perceived threat. Early socialization will ensure that these dogs are well adjusted and do not become fearful or unnecessarily aggressive.

New owners should research their puppy's origins to check that it is from stock with a good temperament. Interbreeding for show success has resulted in structural weaknesses and hip dysplasia. Scrutinize all documentation on testing for inherited diseases before purchasing.

These dogs form close bonds with their owners, and are happiest with people who provide strong leadership together with lots of fun and friendship. Feed their strong desire to work, such as by training them to help out with everyday chores. This will give them a purpose and strengthen your shared relationship.

Muzzle is straight and strong, with firm lips

Hard, straight, outer coat with dense undercoat

Tail is densely feathered with long hair

Chest is deep, with long, well-formed ribs

△ **Coping with the chasing instinct**
Playful and energetic, German Shepherd Dogs love to chase. Channel this strong desire into games with toys, especially if your puppy is growing up with young children. Otherwise, inappropriate chase games can become a bad habit, which will be difficult to break later.

Police dogs

German Shepherds are highly valued by police forces worldwide. Their reactivity and quick arousal assists with detaining criminals, and their natural protectiveness helps to keep the handler safe. Their desire to chase makes them excellent at catching running criminals, and they are strong enough to stop and detain a person until the handler can catch up. Yet with the right socialization and removed from a conflict situation they can also be peaceful and pleasant, which is important for public relations. Their powerful scent-detection abilities allow them to track suspects and also lost persons, as well as to find items that may be used as evidence.

Rhodesian Ridgeback

Height *29.5–38.5kg (65–85lb), 60–69cm (24–27in)*

Character *Independent, discerning, protective*

Exercise *High*

Grooming *Minimal*

Ridgebacks were first bred in South Africa in the late 19th century, and found great success as hunting dogs in Zimbabwe (formerly Rhodesia). Their role was to chase lions in packs, cornering the quarry until the hunters could dispatch it. Like their ancestors, modern Ridgebacks love to chase. This can lead to control problems on walks, and Ridgebacks quickly learn to chase inappropriately, being fond of fast-moving objects and animals. These dogs are affectionate and loyal to owners, and very good with children in the family. They need plenty of early socialization with strangers and other dogs. They love to eat, so food stealing is high on their list of priorities.

Broad, flat skull

Muscular neck

Short, dense, sleek coat

Well-arched toes

△ **The ridge**
This breed's unique feature is the ridge of hair running the wrong way down the back. Tapered near the tail, it ends in two whorls over the shoulders.

Dobermann

Height *30–40kg (66–88lb),60–70cm (24–28in)*

Character *Intelligent, alert, protective*

Exercise *High*

Grooming *Minimal*

The Dobermann was created in the late 19th century by Louis Dobermann, a German tax collector who needed a dog for protection. Dobermanns retain their protective nature, but are easily trained and controllable if they have strong-willed owners. This highly intelligent breed needs plenty to do to use up its considerable energies.

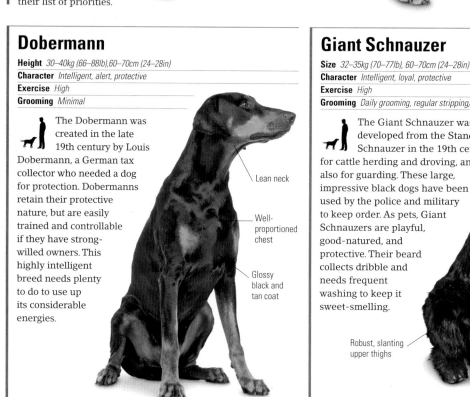

Lean neck

Well-proportioned chest

Glossy black and tan coat

Giant Schnauzer

Size *32–35kg (70–77lb), 60–70cm (24–28in)*

Character *Intelligent, loyal, protective*

Exercise *High*

Grooming *Daily grooming, regular stripping/clipping*

The Giant Schnauzer was developed from the Standard Schnauzer in the 19th century for cattle herding and droving, and also for guarding. These large, impressive black dogs have been used by the police and military to keep order. As pets, Giant Schnauzers are playful, good-natured, and protective. Their beard collects dribble and needs frequent washing to keep it sweet-smelling.

Long, coarse beard

Robust, slanting upper thighs

Weimaraner

Size *32–39kg (70–86lb), 56–69cm (22–27in)*

Character *Energetic, exuberant, playful*

Exercise *Very high*

Grooming *Minimal*

 Weimaraners were developed in Germany as a general-purpose gun dog in the early 19th century. They are still used as gun dogs today, but they are also popular as pets. These fun-loving, extrovert dogs need active families who can include them in all aspects of daily life. Their vast reserves of energy and stamina need channelling into useful work or games with toys. Regular free running and daily off-lead exercise are essential. Strong behavioural guidelines should be set early on; fortunately, Weimaraners are easy to train. Good socialization will ensure that they are friendly to strangers and other animals.

Long-haired Weimaraner

Firm, compact feet

Strong, straight forelegs

Short-coated Weimaraner

Akita

Height *35–50kg (77–110lb), 60–70cm (24–28in)*

Character *Aloof, protective, independent*

Exercise *High*

Grooming *Extensive daily grooming required*

The Akita is an imposing dog, developed for bear hunting and dog fighting in the 17th century. Bred to show little emotion, it is difficult to know what they are thinking, and hence predict what they may do next. They need an experienced owner who can handle their strong character and earn enough respect to be listened to. Akitas can be difficult with other animals and need careful socialization. Clean, quiet, and calm, they make a loving, loyal guard for their families.

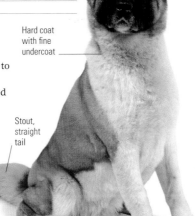

Hard coat with fine undercoat

Stout, straight tail

◁ **Powerful breed**
Akitas are large and powerful. They do not have much interest in play after puppyhood and their independence makes them harder to train. Safe, enclosed areas away from other dogs and animals are needed for exercising.

Dogue de Bordeaux

Height *36–45kg (79–99lb), 58–69cm (23–27in)*

Character *Courageous, loyal, protective*

Exercise *High*

Grooming *Minimal*

This breed probably originated in France's Bordeaux region as a dog for fighting bulls, bears, and other dogs in pits. Subsequently mellowed by selective breeding, the Dogue de Bordeaux today has a less aggressive nature. Nevertheless, it still requires determined owners and early socialization, especially with other dogs. Due to the shape of its jaw and lips, this dog will snore and drool copiously.

Powerful chest

Active dog
Weimaraners have high energy levels and
need plenty of exercise to feel content. As
well as lots of play and activity, they need
safe, open areas where they can run free,
especially when they are young.

Extra-large dogs

Outsize dogs are for experienced, committed owners who can cope with a dog that often weighs more than they do. These breeds are impressive statements, but they make great demands on time and money.

Owners of extra-large dogs need dedication. It will definitely be more expensive to kennel, insure, and feed these dogs, and they will need more time for general care and maintenance. Transport can be a

problem with outsize breeds, and often necessitates the purchase of an extra-large car.

Surprisingly, extra-large dogs do not usually need as much exercise as some of their smaller, more agile cousins. They prefer to take things easy, and quickly get tired from the effort of moving such a large frame. Sadly, these giants tend to be more short-lived than smaller breeds.

◁ **Giant size**
If not well socialized or properly trained, an extra-large dog such as the Great Dane can pose a significant physical risk to others.

▷ **Water dog**
Newfoundlands are used for rescue at sea. Their large size keeps them warm in cold water, and their great strength enables them to pull struggling people to the shore.

Outsize dogs need a lot of house room, and may get in the way or feel too restricted in a small home. They also need a large garden so they can get up to speed and slow down again before reaching the fence.

Leonberger

Height *34–50kg (75–110lb), 65–80cm (26–31in)*
Character *Calm, protective, affectionate*
Exercise *High*
Grooming *Daily grooming required*

First bred by the mayor of Leonberg, Germany, in the 19th century by crossing St Bernards, Newfoundlands, and a few other breeds, Leonbergers became popular as family guard dogs and companions. Though large, they are gentle around familiar children.

Rough, shaggy coat

Bernese Mountain Dog

Height *40–44kg (88–97lb), 58–70cm (23–28in)*
Character *Calm, protective, sociable*
Exercise *Moderate*
Grooming *Daily grooming required*

These dogs were originally bred to work on Swiss farms, where they pulled carts, drove cattle, and acted as guard dogs. Naturally protective, they need good socialization as puppies. Bernese Mountain Dogs are powerful when pulling, so plenty of early lead training is necessary to gain control.

Long muzzle with distinctive markings

Abundant, long, glossy coat

Rottweiler

Height *41–50kg (90–110lb), 58–69cm (23–27in)*
Character *Protective, loyal, alert*
Exercise *High*
Grooming *Minimal*

Rottweilers were bred in Germany to drive cattle and for protection. They need strong-willed, experienced owners to keep their protective instincts in check. Rottweilers are quick to learn, and self-assured.

Coarse, flat black coat with tan markings

Strong forelegs with round, compact feet

Bull Mastiff

Size *41–59kg (90–130lb), 64–69cm (25–27in)*
Character *Courageous, protective, loyal*
Exercise *Moderate*
Grooming *Minimal*

By crossing English Bulldogs and English Mastiffs, English gamekeepers in the 19th century developed the Bull Mastiff to help them catch poachers. Today, these powerful dogs retain their protective nature, and plenty of early socialization, together with thorough training by strong-willed owners, is necessary to rein in these instincts. Despite this, Bull Mastiffs are affectionate with familiar children.

Wide, deep chest

Well-spaced, powerful legs

Great Dane

Height *50–80kg (110–176lb), 79–92cm (31–36in)*
Character *Playful, independent, affectionate*
Exercise *Moderate*
Grooming *Minimal*

Although its exact origins are unclear, this ancient breed was originally developed to hunt wild boar. Today's Great Dane is a gentle giant, one of the tallest of all breeds. It is good-natured and sociable, but care is needed when off-lead, because the desire to chase other animals is strong. Good socialization and training is needed when young.

△ **Fast runners**
Surprisingly fast, Great Danes need large areas where they can exercise freely.

Deep-set eyes

Thick, firm lips

Very deep chest

Short, dense coat

Newfoundland

Height *50–68kg (110–150lb), 66–71cm (26–28in)*
Character *Calm, sociable, affectionate*
Exercise *Moderate*
Grooming *Daily grooming required*

This dog was developed in Newfoundland, Canada, to help fishermen haul nets and carts. The thick coat can cause problems in more temperate climates, and Newfoundlands often seek out water to cool themselves down. They need to pant a lot to lose excess heat, and have a strong tendency to drool. They have a gentle, sociable temperament and make good family dogs.

△ **Keeping cool**
Newfoundlands overheat rapidly if they exercise too much, so short walks are preferable to long marathons. Finding a place where they can swim regularly will keep them fit, cool, and content.

Broad, massive head

Short, square muzzle

St Bernard

Height *50–91kg (110–201lb), 61–71cm (24–28in)*
Character *Gentle, sociable, loyal*
Exercise *Moderate*
Grooming *Daily grooming required*

Bred in the 17th century by the monks at the Hospice of St Bernard in Switzerland, this dog helped to rescue travellers stuck in snow. Its large size reflected the need to stay warm when working for hours in low temperatures. St Bernards are gentle giants, good-natured and devoted to their owners. Often too hot in temperate climates, their panting and excessive dribbling can be a problem.

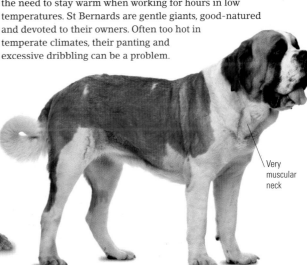

Very muscular neck

Mongrels and crossbreeds

Mongrels and crossbreeds are unique in physical form and temperament. Each dog is different from the next, and you have to wait until they mature to see how puppies will turn out and how big they will grow.

Mongrel dogs are a mixture of different breeds, while crossbreeds are a mixture of two pedigree dogs. Mongrels are common in countries where dogs are allowed the freedom to roam, and where it is unlikely they will be neutered. They are less common in more heavily populated countries where stray dogs are not allowed, and are quickly collected by dog-control officers. Where breeding is taken very seriously, mongrels are usually neutered.

Crossbreeds are usually the result of an accidental mating between two pedigree dogs, but they can be

◁ **Hybrid vigour**
Many mongrels and crossbreeds are healthier than pedigrees, because their genes come from parents that are less likely to be related.

a deliberate cross to try to produce a dog with a particular temperament or coat type. Crossbreeds are usually given a hybrid of the two breed names; for example, a cross between a Cocker Spaniel and a Poodle would be called a Cockerpoo.

◁ **Inherited traits**
The desire to chase and play with toys is an inherited trait. How the dog is raised will affect which behaviour traits are developed.

Canine combinations
You can usually guess at least one of the parents of a mongrel or crossbreed from the clues given by their temperament and body shape. If choosing an adult, what you see is what you get. Find out what character traits the dog has before buying.

▷ **Labradoodles**
To breed assistance dogs that do not shed their coat or trigger people's allergies, Labradors have been crossed with Poodles to produce Labradoodles. These dogs are popular as pets too, and demand for them is increasing. Due to the mixture of genes, various physical forms and types of coat occur.

2

Building bonds

Dog talk

Dogs are not humans in furry skins, but a different species from us. If we are to be good dog owners, we need to be **aware of the differences** between us, and appreciate how the **world looks** from **their perspective**. This section will help you to understand **how dogs think**, and their limitations compared with our own sophisticated abilities to process thoughts. Discover how dogs **"talk"** to each other, and to us, and how we can **communicate** with them using **their language.** It also explains how to **earn your dog's respect** and develop a **happy, trusting relationship** that will provide the framework for creating a **well-behaved, well-trained animal.**

GOOD RELATIONSHIP
Helping children to build a mutually trusting relationship with their dog is beneficial for their development, and also for the dog's well-being

How dogs think

Dogs are highly social, but have less sophisticated thought and reasoning abilities than humans. Knowing how dogs think helps us to understand them and have reasonable expectations of what they can achieve.

Social relationships

A dog's social patterns are very similar to our own. For example, they greet returning members of the pack enthusiastically, they are sad when they lose loved ones, and they work hard to maintain relationships. Parallels in a dog's social life can be seen readily in how we humans behave with our own families.

Shared emotions

Dogs also seem to share many human emotions, including happiness when they are having fun, loneliness when they are separated from their pack, fear when they feel threatened, and resentment if they are told off continuously. Although we cannot

◁ **Warm welcome**
Dogs share our social behaviour of greeting returning loved ones. Having a dog to welcome you home from a hard day's work is one of the joys of dog ownership. However, make sure he does not learn to jump up at you (pp.188–9).

be certain they feel the same way we do, because we cannot ask them, their behaviour in many situations is so similar to ours that it is reasonable to assume that this

is the case. It is because of these shared similarities in social ability and emotional richness that we invite dogs into our homes, where they make very successful pets. However, because they often seem so human, it is easy to make the mistake of treating them like small children and expecting them to behave accordingly.

In reality, dogs have a much less sophisticated brain than humans, and because their ancestors evolved to survive in a different way, their motivations are not the same as ours.

◁ **Infectious mood**
An owner's moods are often reflected in their dog – a happy owner will have a happy dog.

▽ **Lacking logic**
A dog will look at the floor repeatedly when seeing a treat drop, even though there is a table in the way.

▷ **Acute senses**
Using their very keen senses, dogs can often tell when their owners are about to get up even before they consciously decide to move. Thus many owners claim their dogs understand them perfectly and know exactly what they are thinking.

What do dogs feel?

Do dogs feel guilt, remorse, or hatred? Unfortunately, there is no way of asking them, and no scientific experiments have been done to find out. However, it is safe to assume that although they do possess basic emotions, they are unable to process them in a human way. Therefore, they do not hold grudges or plot their revenge. They don't fake emotions for a higher purpose, and if they seem pleased to see you, it is because they genuinely feel that way. It is this inability to show false emotion that makes them so appealing in a modern world filled with deception.

" Dogs are **not small people in furry skins** – they have a much **smaller capacity** for **reasoning and thought** than we do. "

Different brains

Although the dog's brain is similar to that of a human, it is relatively smaller and lacks the neocortex, which is the part of our brain that is responsible for reasoning, language, and all the high-level functions that are unique to humans. Dogs have a good memory, but their reasoning capacity is quite limited when compared with ours. They are acutely aware of human movements and body language, our moods and facial expressions, but most dogs find it really difficult to learn words. This is because a large part of a dog's brain is devoted to processing information from the physical senses, such as smell and hearing (pp.54–7), which detect information about the world around them and evolved to help their wolf ancestors hunt successfully.

Thus dogs are not small "people" in furry skins – they have a much smaller capacity for reasoning and thought than we do, in addition to a different way of seeing the world. Knowing this can help us to have more realistic expectations of their abilities and not ask too much when trying to train them and get them to cooperate with us. Helping our dogs out when they do not understand what we require is vital, as is giving them the benefit of the doubt in those instances when we are not sure if they are being stubborn or just do not know what to do.

▷ **Slow to reason**
In this situation, a dog's first reaction is to try to pull the ball through the fence. In contrast, a human would realize that it is easier to go through the gate in order to pick up the ball.

Canine senses: smell and sight

Dogs experience the world in a very different way to humans. Understanding how they perceive their surroundings helps us to interpret their behaviour and makes training them easier.

Scent

Dogs live in a world of scent, while human beings inhabit a world of sight. We see the world, but dogs smell it. If you watch someone with a dog entering an unfamiliar room, the owner will look around to gain clues as to what goes on in there and what may happen in the future. The dog, however, will put his nose to the ground and move around in order to gather similar information.

Dogs are intensely interested in sniffing, whether it is a smell on the grass, a new object, or the head or rear end of another dog.

△ **Information collection**
This Basset Hound uses his nose to gather information about other dogs in the area, finding out which could be friend, foe, or a potential mate.

"We see the world, but dogs smell it."

This is because they can detect scent on a level we can only imagine. Sniffing a clump of grass can tell them which other dogs inhabit the area, their age, sexual status, state of health, and how long ago they passed by. This is possible because they have an extraordinarily large epithelium (membrane) inside the nose, which collects scent molecules and sends messages to the brain. In addition, the part of a dog's brain that is responsible for scent detection is four times larger and more complex than in humans.

Dogs also have something called a vomeronasal organ in the roof of their mouths. This allows them to taste and smell scents that they find

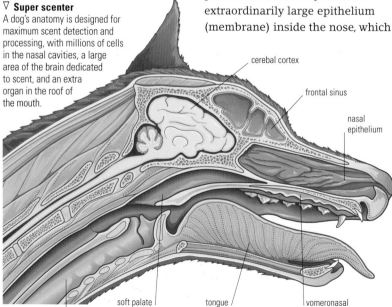

▽ **Super scenter**
A dog's anatomy is designed for maximum scent detection and processing, with millions of cells in the nasal cavities, a large area of the brain dedicated to scent, and an extra organ in the roof of the mouth.

cerebal cortex

frontal sinus

nasal epithelium

windpipe

soft palate

tongue

vomeronasal organ

△ **Crime fighters**
Humans have long capitalized on dogs' superior sense of smell. Here, a sniffer dog checks packages for illegal substances.

especially appealing, particularly those that help them recognize mating partners.

In some breeds – for example, those that are required to do a job that involves tracking or scenting game, such as hounds or gun dogs – we have accentuated this ability through selective breeding. The Bloodhound is probably the breed that is best at scent detection. Dogs can track humans and animals using the trail of skin cells shed from the body and smells caused by disturbance of any vegetation. Dogs are also used to detect explosives, drugs, food, dead bodies, and cancer cells, and they can do this better than any human invention.

Sight

Dogs see less well than humans. Although they can see in colour, the colours they can detect are limited to blues and yellows, and they cannot see reds and greens. This is why they find it difficult to see a red ball on green grass, and

△ **The human's view**
Humans can see texture and detail well and have a much broader range of colour vision than dogs do.

△ **The dog's view**
Dogs can see some colours, but detect texture and detail less well. Their night vision is superior to ours and they detect movements easily.

will often use their sense of smell to search for it instead.

Similarly, dogs cannot distinguish textures and detail as well as we do, but they are better at seeing in the dark, due to a special structure in the eye called the tapetum lucidum. This reflects light back into the dog's eye, enhancing sight in low light levels, and it explains why

dogs' eyes "glow in the dark" when light hits them. Dogs are also able to detect movement better than we can, and many breeds have better long-distance vision.

▽ **Sight hounds**
Some dogs have been bred to hunt by sight. They can detect movements easily and see well at long distances. This Lurcher scans the field for anything that could be chased or hunted.

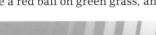

Amazing scent detection

Researchers have estimated that dogs have nearly 220 million cells in their noses that detect scent, covering an area about the size of a handkerchief, compared to five million in humans, which is equivalent to the size of a postage stamp. In scientific experiments, dogs could detect human scent on a glass slide that had been lightly handled even when it was left outdoors for two weeks or indoors for nearly one month. They can successfully detect odours at a concentration of 0.1 part per billion, and are able to follow tracks over 300 hours old. Once on a trail, Bloodhounds have been known to follow it for 210km (130 miles).

Hearing, taste, and perspective

As well as differences in their senses of smell and vision, dogs have very different powers of hearing and taste to humans. Their small height, relative to us, also gives them a very different outlook on the world.

Sounds

The sense of hearing is much better developed in dogs than in humans, and they can hear noises at a much greater distance from the source than we can. Sounds that we can only just hear can be detected by dogs from four times as far away. In addition, they can hear higher frequencies of sound, such as the ultrasonic squeaks made by small prey animals. The frequency range of a dog's hearing is 40–60,000 Hz, whereas we can only hear sounds in the range of 20–20,000 Hz. This is why dogs respond to supposedly "silent" dog whistles, which are only silent to us

because they are beyond the frequency range of our hearing. It was advantageous for dogs that were bred to herd livestock to be able to hear well, so that they could respond to instructions shouted or whistled from some distance away.

◁ **Sound of silence**
A "silent" dog whistle sounds like any other whistle to a dog, but we do not hear it because our ears cannot detect noise at such a high frequency.

For this reason, many of the modern descendants of these dogs have extremely sensitive hearing, and it is not uncommon for herding dogs to develop noise phobias when exposed to loud noises, such as fireworks.

Tastes

Humans have nearly 9,000 taste buds in the mouth, whereas dogs have less than 2,000, so their sense

> ## "For **puppies** and small dogs, **humans must seem like giants.**"

of taste is less sophisticated than ours. Scent is more important than taste to dogs. The taste buds of these carnivores are designed to favour meat and fat, rather than the sweet and salty foods that humans prefer.

A dog's perspective

Being smaller than us, dogs see the world from a different perspective. To find out how life in our homes appears to them, get down on your hands and knees and you will see that it seems a very different place. This is equally true when we take them out in busy towns and cities.

△ **In a land of giants**
For puppies and small dogs, humans are as tall as a double-decker bus. Sometimes this "land of giants" will seem an intimidating place to them.

To dogs, cars seem huge and lorries are like roaring monsters, emitting exhaust gases at nose-height. We often overlook dogs as we hurry through crowded streets, but it is easy to imagine how hard it must be for them to weave their way through a forest of moving legs. For puppies and small dogs, humans must seem like giants. Hands coming down from above may seem threatening to a small dog, especially if he is not sure of our intentions.

Not paws but jaws

Dogs lack delicate fingers and opposable thumbs. Because they need to stand on their paws, manipulating objects has to be done with the mouth. This helps to explain why puppies pick things up with their mouths during exploration, and bite and chew to

◁ **Acquired taste**
Being true carnivores, dogs evolved to enjoy the taste of the raw meat and fat that covered the bones of their animal prey.

△ **Threatening hand**
Always bear in mind how a dog sees you. From a dog's perspective, a huge hand coming down to give a pat on the head can seem very scary.

find out about their world. Unlike human jaws, dog jaws can only move up and down, and they lack the ability to move from side to side.

Sixth sense

Some of the unusual abilities of dogs cause people to wonder if they have a "sixth" sense. For example, there are many recorded incidences of dogs finding their way home over thousands of kilometres. Dogs have also been known to locate their owners even though they have moved to a place the dog has never visited. Even more surprising is the ability of some dogs to predict when their owners are coming home: they will go and wait by the door from the moment the owner sets off for home. It may be that dogs have sensory abilities of which we are not yet aware.

Dog to dog

Because dogs lack the brain structures to learn a verbal language, they communicate using body postures and signals. Learning what dogs are saying to each other requires a careful study of how they hold their bodies.

Although they sometimes bark at each other, most communication between dogs is non-vocal, and involves changes in the positions of their ears, tail, and body. These changes, though small, indicate moods and feelings, and they are used by other dogs as a predictor of future behaviour. To learn this body language, watch what dogs do when they meet. Different personalities behave in different ways, and you will soon be able to predict what will happen next.

"Changes in body position indicate moods and feelings."

△ *"Don't stare"*
This English Setter is trying to get close to investigate by scent, but the firm gaze of the Golden Retriever causes the Setter to look politely away into the distance.

▷ *"Go away!"*
This Weimaraner's boisterous play is too much. To try to turn off the lively attention, the Labrador flattens itself to the ground, keeping still and closing his eyes in a clear signal of disengagement.

Play fight
These dogs know each other well and are playing. Although they are active, there is no sign of tension in their faces or stiffness in their bodies, which would be evident if it were a real fight, and their eyes are not fixated on each other.

◁ **Scent investigation**
The scent of others is an important source of information. Collecting scent from the rear end may be distasteful to us, but it tells dogs a lot about their new canine friends.

▷ **"Please play!"**
The younger dog is lively and playful, with energy to spare. The older dog doesn't want to get involved. In desperation, the younger dog puts his front paws on the back of the older dog to try to provoke a response.

Dog to human

Dogs try to communicate with us using body signals, just as they do with each other. Some signals are easy to recognize, because they have close human equivalents. Others are not so clear, and may be misinterpreted.

Dogs constantly express themselves to us through their body postures. Understanding these signals will enable us to react accordingly and help the dog out if necessary. Remember that dogs are far more vulnerable in the dog–human relationship than we are, as they have less control over what happens to them. Owners should be aware of their dog's sensitivities, and make every effort to learn how to read his signals.

◁ **Nose lick**
Dogs lick their noses when they feel under pressure. This dog leans away, looks worried, and licks his nose when his collar is held.

▽ **Yawning**
Yawning can be a way to ease tension, and it is usually a sign that the dog is anxious or worried. This dog yawns when the owner begins to stare at her.

▽ **Confidence**
A relaxed body and upward-curving tail signals confidence. This young dog is self-assured, and all is well in her world. She shows it by her confident strut and the way she carries her tail.

△ **Avoidance**
This dog is held captive and brought towards the owner's face. He feels overwhelmed by this, so he tries to avoid the owner by turning his head away.

Pleased to see you
This dog has a good relationship with his owner and is confident that her approach means no harm. He wags his tail with excitement, puts his ears down in greeting, and looks up at her with a relaxed expression.

Nose lick
Dogs lick their noses when they are feeling anxious or distressed, or under pressure from their owners. Learning how to read these signals helps you to understand your dog better, and be a better owner.

Human to **dog**

Dogs find it easier to understand our gestures and signals rather than our spoken words. When training them to respond to cues, it is quicker if you teach them hand signals first, and then put a voice cue in later.

Dogs watch us rather than listen to us, as it is not natural for them to communicate vocally. They observe us closely for any clue that we might be ready to do something interesting. For this reason, using gestures to help dogs understand what we want is more likely to succeed than speaking to them. They will, eventually, learn words if we repeat them often enough, but long before that, they will have learned the body gestures that accompany particular requests, and it is to these that they primarily respond.

△ *Wave*
This owner gives a clear hand signal and her well-trained dog responds. If a voice cue is given just before the signal, her dog will eventually learn to respond to the voice cue alone.

◁ *Sit*
"Sit" is often the only voice cue that dogs learn. When this owner gives the voice cue, her well-trained dog sits – even though he cannot see any body cues or signals she may be giving.

△ *Pointing*
With careful teaching, dogs eventually understand that they need to go in the direction in which we are pointing. This dog is not sure, and looks worried.

▽ *What's next?*
Positive training results in a dog that pays attention to your cues, waiting for the next one to tell him what is going to happen or what is required of him. Having a dog that understands our cues makes life much easier – and a lot more fun.

"Dogs watch us rather than listen to us, as it is not natural for them to communicate with words."

△ *Body signals*
This owner sends an obvious "come here" message to her dog with her body language, and her trained dog responds happily. Although it may be obvious to us what we mean, at first dogs have no idea and need to be patiently taught.

A **rewarding relationship**

A good relationship with your dog, which is based on love, trust, and respect, is essential to harmony, good behaviour, and to maximizing his potential in the many different aspects of your life together.

Essential elements

Dogs are pack animals and, as a result, they seek out and rely on their social connections. A special relationship with at least one member of their human family is essential to a dog's wellbeing and good behaviour. If that relationship is strong and solid, the dog will be well-adjusted, more resilient to change or adversity, and better equipped to behave in a way that is acceptable for everyone.

To build this sort of relationship, however, you need to work hard to be loving, trustworthy, and kind. All dogs have a strong sense of injustice, so it is very important to be scrupulously fair in all of your dealings with them. Positive training methods will help to keep your relationship on track as they rely on making your dog want to do as you ask rather than forcing him

△ **Strong bond**
A good social relationship is essential to your dog's wellbeing and will bring contentment and happiness to both of you. However, you have to work at it and put in time and effort.

△ **Establishing trust**
The trust that develops during the formation of a good owner–dog relationship allows you to perform all maintenance tasks easily.

◁ **Working partnership**
Partners in a successful relationship help each other out. Mutual trust and respect will reduce your reliance on rewards when you ask your dog to comply with your wishes, and he will then respond to your requests willingly.

Positive training methods

Positive training, which can be achieved by following the methods that are set out in this book, will enhance your relationship with your dog, and this, in turn, will bring the two of you closer together. As you train, each of you will find out about the other. You will both learn what you are good at, what makes you frustrated, what pleases you, and how each of you can make the other happy. As training continues, and your relationship becomes stronger, you will find that your dog will work harder for you and feel more closely bonded to you. Regular training sessions, especially if they are interspersed with play, will result in your dog becoming a well-trained, well-behaved, willing friend and partner.

to comply. Spending time with him on a regular basis is essential to making him feel loved, wanted, and cared for. If you are too busy to give him the social care that he craves, he may become withdrawn and depressed or exhibit unwanted attention-seeking behaviours.

> **"Dogs benefit** from a **leader** whom they can **respect and follow."**

Bad parenting

Using only positive methods for training, educating, and building a relationship with your dog may be difficult if you were brought up by parents who were very negative towards you, as you may pass this attitude on. It can be difficult to train at times when you are angry or stressed. Although your dog will forgive the occasional slip, prevent damaging your relationship further by avoiding training sessions when you are feeling less positive. A negative approach to training will only lead to resentment and fear.

Leadership

Humans have bred dogs selectively to be sociable and biddable. Because their ancestors once lived in packs, dogs benefit from having a leader that they can respect and follow, and, much like children, they can become unruly and difficult without one. Dogs need to be taught how to behave appropriately, and boundaries of acceptable behaviour need to be set and maintained.

To be an effective leader, you need to be kind and encouraging most of the time, but, when necessary, you must also be tough and uncompromising. Taking the lead by making good decisions about what to do next is an essential leadership quality that your dog will recognize, as is keeping members of your pack safe and leading them out of danger when

▷ **Respect**
Earning your dog's respect is essential if he is to consider you a good leader and always do as you ask without question.

difficult situations arise. Of course, it is possible to force your will on your dog, but he will not regard you as a good leader if you do so – you are more likely to inspire fear. You have to earn your dog's respect through your actions and decisions in daily life. This is the recipe for a good relationship.

Dogs and children

Dogs and children share a sense of fun and a love of life, and they can get along really well together if given the careful supervision needed to ensure good relationships.

Set a good example

Dogs make an ideal pet for children, providing they are carefully supervised to ensure that each behaves well with the other. Leaving them alone together allows all sorts of bad behaviour to flourish and unacceptable habits can quickly develop. Fortunately, children learn quickly. It is relatively easy to teach them how to behave around their dog in order to get the best from him and to develop a successful relationship.

Children also learn from what they observe. They will carefully watch what their parents do with the family dog and will copy this behaviour. For this reason, be extra careful what you do with your dog if the children are watching, because you will see it reflected later.

Children are full of vigour and fun, and well-socialized dogs respond to this with excitement and energy. This makes children very good trainers – if they are shown the correct way to do it. They are usually enthusiastic and excited, too, which brings about a reciprocal

△ **Young trainer**
Children can make skilled and enthusiastic dog trainers given the right information, along with plenty of coaching and support.

◁ **Part of the family**
Children who grow up with a family dog are more likely to keep pet dogs as adults, especially if their experience of dogs is happy and enjoyable.

▽ Happy greeting
Early socialization is essential if puppies are to grow up being friendly to and unafraid of children of all ages. This puppy enjoys the social contact.

excitement from the dog they are training. Success is important, because children quickly get frustrated and impatient if what they try does not work. It is essential to supervise these training sessions, being ready to step in to help out if needed.

Safe play
When playing, children can be unintentionally cruel to dogs, and sometimes they can be intentionally mean if they have been badly treated themselves. If a dog is going to bite, he is statistically more likely to bite young boys in a family. For this reason, all play and interactions between children and the family dog should be supervised in order to avoid getting into a situation where the dog is forced to retaliate.

Children will be readily accepted from a dog's point of view if he met them and had pleasant experiences

with them during early puppyhood (pp.92–3). Young puppies under 12 weeks of age need to meet children of all ages if they are to grow up friendly and unafraid. Otherwise, dogs can be scared of children, particularly toddlers, who appear so different from adults.

Dogs and babies
Babies are usually readily accepted by dogs as new members of the family pack. Even so, it is wise to adjust a dog's routine and social environment during the pregnancy to reflect conditions that will occur after the birth. Playing recordings of babies crying and letting the dog

△ Be there
By supervising play sessions, you can ensure that both your children and your dog enjoy the games, and that both parties learn how to treat each other appropriately.

◁ New pack member
Dogs usually welcome babies as new members of the family pack. It is important to prepare your dog for the new arrival during the pregnancy. Once the baby has arrived, let your dog know he is still a valued member of the household.

get used to the different smells associated with babies will help. Teaching your dog to go to his bed (pp.182–3) is also a good idea, so that you will be able to attend to the baby without interference.

Toddlers
Problems can occur for the family dog when babies start to crawl, move around, and take their first steps. A dog is at risk of being fallen on or grabbed for support. He cannot stop a toddler approaching and needs to learn to move to specially created "safe havens", out of the way. With their big eyes at dog eye level, unsteady gait, loud squeaks and cries, and pinching fingers, toddlers can seem threatening. Care needs to be taken until the baby has grown, and child and dog are used to each other.

"Children can make very good trainers if they are shown the correct way to go about it."

Dogs and other animals

Dogs who are socialized with other animals from an early age tolerate them well and can be friendly. Care must be taken around small animals, however, as dogs have strong inherited tendencies.

Meeting other animals

Adult dogs will try to be friendly with members of any species they have met during their critical socialization period, which is before they are 12 weeks of age. As they age, they become less inclined to be sociable, and any animals not encountered during puppyhood will be met with caution and alarm.

If a puppy is going to live with or be in contact with other species, it is vital that he meets them as early as possible, especially if he is required to be relaxed and happy in their company. During these meetings, it is important that the puppy has pleasant encounters with other animals, because meeting an aggressive animal can rapidly cause a puppy to become fearful and aggressive in turn.

Predatory instincts

As well as early socialization, dogs need continued supervision when in the presence of small animals so that excitement doesn't escalate into predatory behaviour.

Dogs are descended from wolves, and so they retain many of the traits that are useful for hunting (pp.18–9). Some breeds are more difficult than others in this respect.

△ **Natural chaser**
Care needs to be taken with small, vulnerable pets, such as the rabbit shown here. Dogs should never be trusted completely because their hunting instincts are strong.

"Dogs' **instincts** are **strong** and **should not** be **underestimated**, especially when they are around small, **vulnerable pets**."

△ **Height advantage**
Cats feel safer if they have a higher "escape route". Providing cats with safe places will allow them to get to know the dog more quickly.

▷ **Controlled encounter**
Take time to get your puppy accustomed to livestock, such as chickens, in a controlled way. This takes away the excitement of future encounters.

△ **Controlled encounters**
Keeping your dog under control while in fields of livestock and horses is important to prevent the dog from giving chase – or the other animals from chasing and injuring your dog.

Those whose immediate ancestors were bred to kill vermin (the terriers), those that were bred to chase (the herding dogs), and any others with a strong predatory instinct are much more likely to be troublesome to other animals than those bred as companions.

Care should always be taken with small pets such as hamsters, gerbils, rabbits, and birds. It is surprising how quickly a dog can turn from a calm pet to an aroused killer when little creatures scurry around them or fly off suddenly. Their instincts are strong and should not be underestimated, especially when they are around small, vulnerable pets.

Chasing games

Some animals are more likely to be chased than killed, but this behaviour can potentially get dogs – and their owners – into trouble. Horses, for example, are large and, if unfamiliar to the dog, can represent a serious challenge that the dog may decide to scare away. All kinds of livestock are potential chase targets for an inexperienced, untrained dog.

The likelihood of traffic accidents, damage to property, and potential injury to other animals, as well as to the dog, is high when dogs chase out of control. For these reasons, owners should do all they can to avoid this behaviour.

This can best be done by accustoming puppies to livestock, horses, cats, and other smaller pets from an early age. Sitting with them under control in a place where they can experience these animals will teach puppies to relax and to behave well with them in the future.

This process can take longer with adult dogs, but they, too, will gradually learn to accept other animals if you can find enough time to train them to do so.

Dogs and cats

If cats and dogs grow up together, they can learn to tolerate, and even enjoy, each other's company. If he has never lived with one, however, the family dog may be aggressive to a new kitten or cat and try to chase it out of the house, particularly if he is a terrier. Time is important. All you can do is make both animals feel as comfortable and safe as possible, giving each time and space to find their feet, and not forcing encounters until they are ready to make friends.

What your dog needs

Learning **what your dog requires** for a fulfilling life is key to being a good owner. If you can **meet** these **needs,** you will help him to be **content** and thus **easy to live with.** Making sure your dog **feels safe** in his world will allow him to relax and prevent him from showing defensive behaviour. Giving him enough opportunities to **play and exercise,** and providing the correct **nutrition,** will make him feel comfortable and increase his sense of **well-being**. This section tells you how to achieve this, as well as looking at **grooming and handling,** and the complex issue of **breeding and neutering.**

COAT CARE
Keeping the coat free from tangles and in good condition is an important part of providing for your dog's needs.

Safety

Dogs need our help to allow them to feel safe in our world, and also to avoid all the unwanted behaviours that arise when they feel the need to defend themselves against actual or perceived threats.

Staying safe

In our world, humans always take priority and dogs have to go along with our decisions. Because dogs cannot speak our language, they cannot ask us for help or tell us when they are frightened. Nor can they complain or write us a note when they are anxious or worried.

▽ **Flight**
Dogs usually move away from a threat if it is possible to do so. This dog holds back his ears and walks away looking tense.

When a dog feels under threat and afraid, its fear is evident in the way that the dog holds its body. If the dog's owner does not see this or does not know how to interpret these signs, the dog will continue to feel afraid and, when it feels really threatened, it will have no choice but to defend itself. Owners often view any growls and snaps as unacceptable behaviour, and they may punish their dog in an attempt to stop it. However, this

"If a dog is afraid, he cannot think of anything other than getting safe."

reaction only serves to create confusion in the dog, leading to yet more anxiety and concern.

As in all animals, safety is always of paramount importance for dogs;

if a dog is afraid, he cannot think of anything other than making himself safe. Indeed, he will not be able to eat, play, or concentrate. He may snatch at offered treats and then spit them out.

Courses of action

A dog who is threatened has four options, which are as follows:
■ Freeze – keep perfectly still and hope that he will be left alone.
■ Appease – attempt to show a bigger animal he means no harm.
■ Flight – run away from danger.
■ Fight – use aggression to get rid of the threat.

Help your dog feel safe

To prevent your dog feeling fearful, you need him to be comfortable and familiar with everything that he may encounter in his world. Good socialization during puppyhood (pp.92–3) will produce a well-adjusted dog who views the outside world as a safe place.

A good relationship with his owner is an essential element in a dog's sense of safety. If he trusts his owner, he is more likely to trust and feel safe with other humans.

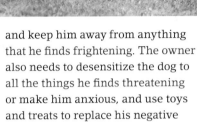

▷ **Appease**
This dog adopts a submissive posture when faced with a stranger. Puppies and gentle dogs often use this strategy.

▽ **Fight**
Eyes wide, ears back, and teeth on show, this dog gives a threat display in an attempt to make a stranger move away.

Positive training and education from owners will help to reinforce this. It is also important to protect a dog from bad experiences, and owners should make sure that their dog is feeling comfortable and safe at all times.

With a dog who has not undergone good early socialization, or who has had bad experiences and is already scared, the owner must learn to read the dog's body language (pp.60–1)

◁ **Protect him**
Carefully expose puppies to new experiences while they are still young and receptive. This owner helps her puppy to get used to traffic by being supportive and cheerful, to encourage a positive attitude in her dog.

and keep him away from anything that he finds frightening. The owner also needs to desensitize the dog to all the things he finds threatening or make him anxious, and use toys and treats to replace his negative feelings with positive experiences.

Owners of dogs that are already aggressive should seek help from an experienced pet behaviourist (p.254), who can give an accurate diagnosis and prepare a treatment plan to help change your dog's behaviour. They can also help with dogs that are not yet aggressive, but may become so without treatment.

Aggression

Dogs only use aggression when they have no other option. If they are cornered or on a lead, they cannot use the flight option, the freeze option is not working, and so they have no choice. Dogs will usually growl in an attempt to make the threat back off. They may bark aggressively and snap in the air, lunging quickly with lots of noise to try to scare the threat away. If a threat appears too suddenly, with no time for warnings, dogs may bite. Biting is usually a last resort when all else has failed. Dogs tend to be very distressed afterwards, and will be relieved if their owners help them find a non-aggressive solution to their problem.

Exercise requirements

A well-exercised dog is calm and easy to live with. On the other hand, a dog that is kept restricted and confined readily becomes a boisterous, agitated nuisance who is really difficult to own.

Harnessing energy

Dogs have inherited the genes that give them the desire to run and be active from their ancestors and wild relatives, wolves, who need to keep their bodies in good condition for hunting. These active traits have been deliberately enhanced through selective breeding to produce breeds with great energy and stamina for different types of work.

In our modern world, many owners can only spare a relatively small amount of time for their dogs. In addition, most dogs are no longer worked. This often results in pet dogs having too much energy for

△ **Retrieving**
Teaching a puppy to retrieve toys is essential if you want to be able to exercise him quickly and easily when he is older.

▷ **Walking**
Walking should be an essential part of your routine as it will provide exercise, mental stimulation, and interest for both of you.

their owners to cope with, especially the descendants of working dogs.

Problem behaviours are common in under-exercised dogs, as they try to find an alternative outlet for their considerable mental and physical energies. Dogs with too much energy may chew all sorts of

> **"** If you have **limited time to spend with your dog** each day, you need to **make the most of it. "**

△ **Burning energy**
Free-running exercise is essential. It not only makes dogs feel good, but also they are much nicer to live with when they return home.

household goods, chase away imaginary intruders whenever they hear a sound, steal things, become obsessed with finding food, bark, whine, and run away in search of entertainment. They jump up, are boisterous and thoughtless, and find it difficult to concentrate on learning or pleasing their owners. If you have only a limited time to spend with your dog each day, you need to make the most of it. Dogs

need both physical exercise and mental stimulation. Physical exercise should be aerobic, in the form of free running and play, and stamina-building, as is the case with walking. Teach your dog to come back when called (pp.124–5) and also to retrieve (pp.136–41), so that he is reliable off the lead and can be exercised easily. Short sessions of vigorous play, interspersed with periods of walking and off-lead running, will give you the ideal exercise plan.

How much is enough?

The amount of exercise you give depends on your dog and his needs. Two daily walks of about an hour's duration each are enough for a healthy, young working dog, but older dogs and those from non-working stock will need less. As well as physical exercise, dogs require mental exercise, in the form of playing and learning. Make time to teach your dog different games and actions, so that you can exercise his mind easily while at home without exhausting yourself. Finding hidden objects in boxes or around the house is a good mental exercise

(pp.172–3). Learning new tricks (pp.160–85) and exercises will keep him active and involved in your everyday life, with the advantage that he will be tired when you want to rest or have to go out to work.

Puppies

Puppies need careful exercise, as they have soft joints and bones that cannot tolerate too much walking. Active play and free running for short periods will help to use up their energy and make them easier to raise. Puppies and young dogs often have a "mad five minutes", when they race around crazily with their tail tucked underneath them.

△ **Regular lessons**
Learning new exercises and tricks uses up your dog's mental energy, and gives you useful cues that you can use to involve him in your daily life.

Nutrition

What a dog eats can make a difference to his state of health and his ability to fight off disease, as well as to how he feels and behaves.

Building bonds

The right diet

Just like humans, dogs need foods that give them energy and nutrients. A balanced dog food should contain the following:

- Fats
- Proteins
- Carbohydrates
- Minerals
- Vitamins
- Water

Dogs need the correct ratio of fat to proteins as well as all 10 essential amino acids, essential fatty acids, minerals, and vitamins. While a home-prepared diet can contain all of these, many owners prefer the easier option of buying a complete food from pet-food manufacturers that has been specially prepared to provide balanced nutrition.

The disadvantages of prepared foods are that they often contain artificial preservatives and can contain chemicals to provide colour and flavour. In addition, all the food is pre-cooked before packing, which may rob it of some of its nutrients. The advantages are that these foods are very convenient and, if you buy from a well-established, reputable company, you can be sure that the food contains all your dog needs for a balanced diet.

Some owners prefer to feed a more natural diet of raw meat and bones with liquidized vegetables and other supplements. The advantages are that this method of feeding is more natural and no preservatives are needed.

▷ **Feeding for health**
What you feed your dog could affect how long he lives, how well he is, and how he behaves. Always provide him with a balanced diet.

"Always make any changes in your dog's diet gradually to avoid upsetting his digestion."

Dog-food types

The range and choice of dog food has expanded greatly during the last few decades. Not only can you now choose from "complete" dry mixes or moist tinned ones, but there are also sachets of "natural" or organic ready-made foods, as well as specially developed mixes tailored to the differing nutritional needs of puppies and older dogs ("seniors"). Many owners prefer to feed a home-made diet of raw foods known as the BARF diet (the letters stand for Bones And Raw Food, or Biologically Appropriate Raw Food), which is claimed to be healthier because it is uncooked. However, home-made diets do need to be carefully balanced.

Complete dried dog food   Sachet   Senior

Tinned   BARF diet   Puppy

Bones and chewing

Puppies chew when teething. If given the opportunity, adult dogs will continue to chew throughout their lives to keep their jaws and teeth in good condition. There is much controversy over what dogs should chew. Some vets advise against bones because they can cause intestinal trouble. If you allow bones, never feed cooked ones (these can splinter), and remove the bone from your dog before he ingests too much. Pet shops sell a variety of smoked and hardened bones, together with rawhide chews and a range of other types (pp.94–5).

The disadvantages are that it is time-consuming and it is difficult to ensure that a balanced diet is being provided.

Diet and behaviour

There is limited scientific evidence for the effects of diet on behaviour. Food that seems to suit one dog may appear to cause another to be difficult and badly behaved. As well as behaviour therapy, it is sometimes worth changing the diet to see if this improves matters. If your dog is showing unwanted behaviour half an hour after eating, every time he eats,

he may be allergic to the food. Consult your veterinary surgeon about what to feed. Always make changes in diet gradually to avoid upsetting your dog's digestion.

Energy requirements

Different dogs have different energy requirements. For example, a nursing mother needs more energy to feed her puppies, a working dog needs more energy to keep going all day, a dog in cold conditions needs more energy to keep warm, and a neutered dog needs less energy than one that is entire. For this reason, always be prepared to vary the amount fed to keep your dog at his ideal weight

(see diagram below). If you are doing a lot of training, remove some of his daily ration each day to allow for extra treats that will be given during the training sessions.

▷ **Over-eating**
Feeding your dog too much will compromise his health and make it more difficult for him to play and exercise. Adjust his food intake accordingly.

▷ **An ideal weight**
Just like humans, a dog's optimal weight should be neither too thin nor too fat. Extremes either way compromise health.

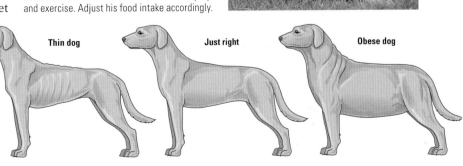

Thin dog   Just right   Obese dog

Why dogs play

For wild dog puppies, play is a rehearsal for the hunting behaviours they need later in life in order to survive. Domestic dogs play throughout their lives, and they incorporate many aspects of the hunting sequence.

Natural behaviour

Both wolf and domestic dog puppies begin to play various hunting and wrestling games as soon as they are sufficiently coordinated. This play strengthens their bodies and allows them to practise all the moves they need for hunting, so they can become proficient while still being fed by others. Although our domestic dogs have no need to catch their own food, the instincts that allow them to do so are often still present, and puppies need to find an outlet for these natural behaviours. Consequently, they practise following moving objects, stalking, chasing, and pouncing, becoming more efficient as they grow and hone their skills.

Types of games

Dogs play three types of games with us: chase games, tug-of-war games, and squeaky toy games.

Chase This is the most widely played game. If you teach your dog how to bring back a toy to you (pp.138–9), it is a great way to exercise him without expending too

◁ **Thrill of the chase**
Herding dogs love the thrill of the chase and can become completely obsessed with chasing toys. Play frequently to use up energy, but keep sessions short to avoid exhausting your dog.

> **"Play strengthens their bodies and** allows them to **practise** all the moves **they will need for hunting."**

081

◁ **Tugging game**
Tug games are great fun for dogs, especially terriers and competitive dogs, but they do need strict rules to prevent them getting out of hand.

▽ **Disinterested**
Dogs of some breeds, especially hounds, are not very interested in playing with toys. Moving the toy, like small prey, can stimulate their interest.

much energy yourself. Some breeds enjoy chase games more than others, especially herding dogs, which were bred to enjoy the chase, and gun dogs, which were developed to pick things up and thus are natural retrievers.

If your dog is a very enthusiastic player, who will run again and again, take care not to overheat him on hot days with too much running. Always play in short, active bursts, and then give him sufficient time to cool down in between sessions.

Tug of war Terriers and other strong-willed dogs enjoy tug-of-war games. For some dogs, this is their favourite game and they will try to play it even if it means hanging on to their owner's sleeve or their lead. Since tugging is a vigorous game, which is played in close proximity to your dog, you must establish some practical rules for play:
■ Only allow play with toys – not with your sleeves or trouser legs.
■ Your dog should stop tugging as soon as you ask him to.

△ **Killer instinct**
Squeaky toys are exciting to predatory dogs, who enjoy "killing" the squeak. However, once it no longer squeaks, the toy is usually discarded.

■ Be sure to win tug-of-war games more often than you lose them.
■ The game must end immediately if any connection is made between the dog's teeth and human skin.
■ Always remove the toy at the end of the game and put it away.

Squeaky toy games Dogs with a strong predatory instinct, especially terriers, enjoy playing with squeaky toys, as the squeak represents the cry of an injured animal. Repellent though this may appear to us, it is just a game to our dogs. Some dogs can keep a squeaky toy intact for a long time, whereas others work fast to destroy the squeak inside the toy and then instantly lose interest.

Non-players
Not all dogs are natural toy players; instead, they prefer to chase live animals if the opportunity arises. Most hounds fall into this category. Trying to get them to play with toys after puppyhood is difficult, but it can be achieved if you can make the toy move like small prey. Be patient, and keep games fun and active.

Toys on a walk

If your dog likes to chase, always remember to take some toys with you when you go for a walk, so that you can play together. If he is focused on playing with you, he is less likely to run off looking for other things to chase and to get into trouble chasing other dogs, joggers, cyclists, livestock, and cars. Taking toys on a walk will also help prevent the temptation to throw sticks for your dog. Vets treat many cases in which the end of a stick has stuck in the ground and an enthusiastic dog has injured his mouth on the other end.

◁ **Exercise props**
Dogs who enjoy playing with toys are much easier to exercise, especially if they learn how to bring the toy back to you after the chase.

Fit for life
Providing good nutrition, plenty of exercise, and everything else your dog requires will make him contented and pleasant to live with. He will also be easier to train and will learn more quickly.

Well behaved play

Teaching an adult dog to play is easy, but you will need patience and perseverance. When dogs begin to play with toys, teaching them good play manners will prevent any accidents caused by over-excitement.

Teach your dog to play

Most dogs want to play, but some may not have played with their owners as puppies and do not know how to play with toys. Others, who may have been told off for picking up objects in the past, may be reluctant to take hold of toys.

Choose a time to play with your dog when he is already excited. Begin with a small fluffy toy. Holding one end, move it along the floor erratically. Keep it moving, sometimes hiding it behind furniture and at other times revealing it quickly before hiding it again. As your dog becomes interested and comes to investigate, move the toy towards him quickly and then pull it away again to tempt him. As he closes in on it for the second or third time, let him take it and play with it for a few seconds

△ **Edible incentive**
Encourage a reluctant dog to get interested in a toy by hiding food inside. Chasing the toy to get the food teaches him that toys are fun.

> **"When** your dog plays **enthusiastically,** you can begin **teaching** him **good manners."**

before moving it away and repeating the exercise. Continue in this way, keeping the lessons short, until your dog's tail starts to wag in anticipation of a game whenever he sees the toy. If you have difficulty in getting him interested in the toy, tempt him with tasty food treats tucked inside it. Let him sniff the toy before throwing it just out of his reach. As he goes to investigate, encourage him to pick up the toy and, if necessary, help him get the food out and praise him well.

Good manners

When your dog plays well and enthusiastically, you can begin to teach him good manners. Control measures will always help to reduce his enthusiasm, so be sure to wait until he is playing really well before you embark on this stage.

The three rules

To instil good manners, you must teach your dog to do the following:
■ Sit and wait patiently when you have a toy until you let him know that you are ready to start play.

◁ **Puppy play**
Young puppies are easily enticed to play. They prefer soft toys, especially when teething.

△ **Retain control**
You need to teach your dog to stop and let go of a toy as soon as you ask him. This prevents over-excitement and teaches self-control.

his mouth by offering a tasty treat instead. Praise him for letting go of the toy and then decide if you want to play again. If he will not relinquish the toy, keep everything as still as possible to avoid any excitement, and wait until he makes his own decision to stop holding on to the toy. Reward him enthusiastically when he does.

Benefits of playing games

Playing games with your dog brings many benefits, helping build close bonds, preventing him finding other outlets for his energy, and keeping him fit. Play his favourite game by choosing whichever toy interests him most, and use different toys to introduce variety. Ensure that both of you are having fun, and keep the games as light-hearted as possible.

■ Keep his teeth well away from your hands during the game.
■ Stop playing as soon as you tell your dog to do so.
Teaching these three rules will ensure that all games are played in a controlled way and with no risk of damage to you. To teach your dog to keep his teeth off you during play, simply stop and walk away

△ **Play request**
Enthusiasm for games takes a while to develop, but once an adult dog has learnt how to play, he will usually want to do so frequently.

from him if his teeth touch you, so that he learns to be more careful next time. To teach him to stop playing on command, ask him to stop and then bring the game to a swift close, removing the toy from

Grooming and handling

Grooming and handling sessions with your dog allow you to carry out essential body maintenance procedures. They also provide an opportunity to give your social dog the love and affection he needs.

The need to touch

Dogs rarely touch each other unless they are playing, fighting, or mating. Humans need to touch their dogs, not only to restrain them and carry out essential activities, but also to show their affection. Dogs must learn to trust that we will not hurt them in this process.

Handling should begin when your dog is a puppy, although adult dogs can still be taught to accept these

▽ **Massage session**
Everyday handling, grooming, and massaging sessions with your dog will help to build trust and enhance the special bond between you.

procedures if you allow sufficient time for them to learn to trust you. Always keep handling sessions short and friendly, and be patient, adopting a gentle approach. Move slowly until your dog accepts what you are doing, and make sure he is fully relaxed before you move on to the next stage.

Restraint

Dogs not only need to learn that in handling them we mean them no harm, but also that they cannot get free until we let them go. This is important, as a dog who cannot be

△ **Avoid a struggle**
Teaching your dog to accept and even enjoy gentle restraint will make him a better patient if he ever becomes sick or is injured in an accident.

effectively handled will be difficult to treat if he is sick or injured. Gradually get your dog used to being held and restrained – don't press your fingers into him, but gently and firmly hold on if he tries to move away. Release him when he is still and relaxed.

Grooming

Some breeds need more grooming than others, but all will benefit from daily examination and handling. A natural coat is made up of an insulating under-layer of short, fluffy hair, with coarser protective hairs on top to keep out wind and rain. Selective breeding has resulted in a variety of coat types, which require different grooming routines. Some moult naturally, some need clipping, and others need to have the old hairs stripped out by hand. Whatever your dog needs, ensure he enjoys these sessions and be considerate when you use brushes and combs.

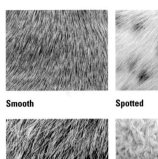
Smooth

Spotted

Rough

Wiry

Curly

Long

◁ **Coat types**
Coat types vary according to a dog's breed, and each will need a different care routine to keep the coat in good condition. Long and curly coats require the most care.

Nail clipping

It is a good idea to get this done by an experienced person at a veterinary surgery or grooming parlour to avoid cutting the quick, which ends close to the end of the nail and carries blood vessels and nerves. Get your dog used to the feel of the clippers against his nails, and having his paws held.

Bathing

A dog's oily coat, there to protect him against the elements, often gets dirty and smelly. If your dog is kept inside and is well sheltered from harsh weather conditions, there is no reason not to wash him as often as you like. However, make sure that he enjoys it, and dry him thoroughly afterwards.

△ **Keeping trim**
Dogs with long, silky hair need daily grooming to keep them free of knots, as well as regular trips to the grooming parlour.

The power of touch

Once your dog has got used to being handled, he will enjoy grooming and massage. Use these sessions as an opportunity for a quick health check to find any parasites, lumps, cuts, or abnormalities that may need veterinary attention.

△ **Mind the quick**
Take care to avoid cutting the quick that runs through the centre of the nail. Ask a veterinary surgeon, nurse, or a professional dog groomer to show you what to do or ask them to do it for you.

Grooming tools

There are a wide variety of grooming tools available to suit all coat types. Choose those that are appropriate for keeping your dog's fur free of mats and knots. If your dog has a long or curly coat, seek advice from a professional dog groomer.

Brushes and combs
These perform different functions, and the ones you choose depends on your dog's coat length and type.

Slicker brush

Bristle brush

Fine-toothed comb

Breeding and neutering

The decision of which dogs will mate and produce puppies is largely controlled by humans. Owners need to decide whether to have their dog neutered or cope with living with an entire (un-neutered) animal.

Responsible ownership

Life with an entire dog, male or female, is more complicated than living with a neutered pet – the behaviours that facilitate mating can cause problems if they are not properly managed. If accidental mating does occur, you will have to find good homes for the resulting puppies. Careful thought should be given to producing a litter and, if this is not desired, you should consider the benefits of neutering.

Entire male dogs

Entire males are always intensely interested in other dogs within their territory, and therefore they spend a considerable time investigating scent marks to verify the reproductive status of females and also to check out the competition from other entire males.

If entire male dogs scent a female who is ready to mate, they will mark their territory more, become more competitive with other males, and work hard to track the female down. The desire to reproduce is strong, and entire males with mating in mind are unlikely to listen to their owners' commands. Some dogs may even be difficult to confine at home, howling, going off their food, and mounting people's legs, cushions, and other "suitable" objects.

△ **Scent marking**
The hormone testosterone triggers changes in a male dog's brain at puberty, causing him to lift his leg when he urinates and allowing him to scent mark objects more accurately.

▽ **Roaming**
If an entire male dog picks up the scent of a female in season, he may escape from home, or run off on walks, to try to track her down.

▷ New lives
Finding good homes for a litter of puppies is not an easy task. They will also need veterinary care, good food, regular cleaning, and plenty of socialization as they develop.

▽ Female rivalry
Entire females living in the same household can develop intense rivalry during oestrus, leading to bullying or fights.

Entire female dogs

Entire females come into oestrus about once every six months for two weeks. During this time they are sexually receptive to the advances of entire males. They have mood changes, may fight with other females, and may even try to escape to find a mate. If they are not mated, they can experience phantom pregnancies about two months later, when they make nests, produce milk, and look after phantom or substitute babies.

Neutering

Neutering involves the surgical removal of the dog's reproductive organs by a vet under anaesthesia. It takes away the desire to mate and all the associated behaviours. It is usually carried out at puberty for males and after the first season for females, although it can be done earlier or later. For entire females that are not required for breeding, it reduces the risk of possible life-threatening womb infections and mammary tumours. However, there is an increased risk of urinary incontinence in neutered bitches. Disadvantages for both sexes involve coat changes and increased appetite, which can lead to weight gain unless food is restricted. Neutering only removes desires that are prompted by circulating sex hormones, and it is not a cure-all for behaviour problems.

Inherited diseases

Selective breeding to produce the perfect show dog has resulted in a reduction of the number of mates available, and parents are often too closely related. This increases the risk of inherited disease, so before buying a puppy, check his parents have been tested and found to be free of disease. Testing for inherited diseases, and discarding diseased stock from breeding dogs, is essential for producing healthy puppies and eradicating future health problems.

"Life with an **entire dog** is **more complicated** than living with a neutered pet.**"**

▷ Removing urges
A neutered dog is more content to stay at home with its owner, not needing to escape and run off to track down a suitable mate.

Age-related issues

Each stage of canine life brings with it different **challenges** and responsibilities. **Puppyhood** is the most time-consuming and important stage – the **habits** formed and **behaviour patterns** learned in the first year will last a lifetime. **Adolescence** is a **testing time** for owners, and issues needs to be worked through carefully. **Elderly dogs** need **special care** to help them live contentedly and cope with the **difficulties** that **old age brings.** This section will prepare you for the **challenges ahead,** giving you the information you need to **help your dog progress through life with ease.**

LIFE'S LESSONS
Puppyhood is a time for finding out about the world, for building good habits, and for learning about how to live with humans.

Puppyhood: the first year

The first year of a dog's life sets its character and forms its behavioural habits. The traits it develops may be good or bad depending on the effort made by the breeder and the puppy's new owner.

Socialization

One of the main influences on a puppy's adult character is the amount of socialization he receives during the first 12 weeks of his life. During these crucial weeks, puppies will readily make friends with humans and other animals – good experiences around both are vital during this period.

Lack of exposure to people and pets at a young age may cause a puppy to be fearful and shy in

cars, steps, slippery surfaces, and loud noises. For these reasons, it is essential that your puppy is born and raised in a household rather than outside in a kennel. Breeders and owners alike must ensure that puppies meet – and have pleasant encounters with – as many new people as possible during their early lives, and that they experience a wide range of stimulating environments. This process should continue until they reach maturity.

Good habits

As well as socialization, puppies need to be well educated throughout the first 12 months, to ensure they grow up into well-behaved and well-adjusted adult dogs. Good habits established during this critical period will last a lifetime, as will bad ones.

Puppies always require constant supervision to ensure they make

△ **Gentle exposure**
Gradually introducing your puppy to everyday objects will help him feel safe and comfortable, and his world will seem a less frightening place.

the right choices. For owners, just being there to educate and train them is as important as doing the right thing. Reward-based training, following the examples shown in this book, will enable you to train reliable responses, as well as develop a good relationship with your dog, based on love and trust.

△ **Character building**
Happy encounters with all types of people and animals are essential for developing a friendly, well-adjusted character in a young puppy.

unfamiliar situations, for example with children and other animals. This fearfulness can develop into aggressive behaviour as the puppy grows into an adult.

In addition, a young puppy needs to get accustomed to its environment and become familiar with the wide range of everyday occurrences inside and outside the home, including vacuum cleaners,

▷ **Reward good behaviour**
Teaching your puppy what he should do is both easier and kinder than telling him off for doing things that you don't want him to do.

"A **puppy** should be **born and raised** in a **household** rather than in a **kennel.**"

Setting boundaries

It is equally important to set boundaries so that your puppy learns what is and is not acceptable. Puppies are eager to please until they reach adolescence, so utilize this time to teach them what they can and should not do. Making your puppy aware that he cannot have everything his own way will help him learn to deal with the frustration he will face later in life when he wants something he cannot have. Teaching him that you will not give way once you have decided on a course of action will let him know that you are mentally stronger than him, and will prevent him from making challenges later on. If you win lots of small contests now, he is less likely to challenge you over more important issues when he is bigger and stronger.

△ **Ignore bad behaviour**
Always make a point of ignoring any form of unwanted behaviour. Never reward it. Once your puppy learns that he will not be rewarded for this behaviour, he will stop doing it.

▷ **Distraction technique**
If the behaviour is self-rewarding, such as stealing food from the table, prevent it by using a lead and a toy and distracting your puppy into doing something more acceptable instead.

Solutions to puppy problems

Puppies do not arrive in our homes already trained. Not only do we need to teach them carefully how to behave, but we also have to tackle any behaviour problems early on to prevent them becoming bad habits.

Play biting

This is one of the most common puppy problems. Playful puppies bite our hands and sometimes our arms, faces, and feet in an attempt to get us to play with them. This is quite normal for them as they play with other members of their species by biting and wrestling, but when they do it to us, their very sharp puppy teeth hurt and therefore this form of play is unacceptable. For this reason, we need to teach them to play with toys instead.

During the early days with your puppy, always have a large soft toy to hand when you interact. Move it and wriggle it, keeping the rest of your body still, so that the toy becomes something exciting for the puppy to chase and grab. Play gently, letting him take the toy sometimes, and if you have children encourage them to do the same. Once your puppy learns how to play with toys and can do so successfully, he will stop play biting.

Chewing

Chewing is another normal behaviour for teething puppies. Providing plenty of items that can be chewed is the secret to getting through this phase without too many ruined shoes and other household items. Supervise your

△ **Toy play**
Teaching your puppy to play with toys instead of your hands will prevent him practising play biting as well as providing an outlet for his strong desire to play games with you.

◁ **Play biting**
Puppies try to get us to play by biting our hands in the same way they play with their siblings. If this happens, remove your hand and end the game.

Types of chew

There are many different chews on the market, ranging from traditional rawhide types to sterilized, stuffed, and smoked bones. Squeeze some edible treats into a strong toy with holes in it, or into a sterilized bone. Extracting the treats will keep your puppy busy and prevent him from chewing other household items. It also helps to channel and use up his strong drive to chew.

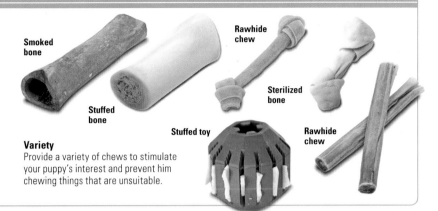

Smoked bone

Stuffed bone

Rawhide chew

Sterilized bone

Stuffed toy

Rawhide chew

Variety
Provide a variety of chews to stimulate your puppy's interest and prevent him chewing things that are unsuitable.

puppy when he is in places where these things may be lying around, and make sure there are plenty of suitable appetizing chews available.

However, puppies soon get bored and may be tempted by items they should not chew. Deal with this by offering a variety of chews every few days, taking away the old ones and bringing out different ones, so that there is always something new to investigate and chew. Beware of another chewing phase at around seven to ten months as your puppy becomes a growing adolescent.

House training

Toilet training is easy if you are vigilant as puppies are born in a nest and come ready programmed to be clean. Help them to learn that the whole house is their nest by always taking them outside at the following times:
■ Soon after each feed.
■ After playing, exercise, and any excitement.
■ On waking from a sleep.
■ First thing in the morning and last thing at night.
■ At least once every hour.
Stay outside with your puppy, or he will be too lonely to concentrate, and let him run about and sniff. If you supervise your puppy

△ **Finding a good spot**
Stay out with your puppy when he needs to go to the toilet. Your reassuring presence will help him relax and go more quickly than if he is left alone.

constantly during the first two weeks, and take him outside whenever he looks like he may need to go to the toilet, he will have fewer accidents and house training will progress very quickly.

Puppy classes

Taking your puppy to a training class not only improves your skills and techniques, but also socializes him with other puppies and people. Ensure the trainer uses positive methods and avoid classes where puppies or people are treated badly. Go to classes specifically for puppies under 20 weeks. A small

▷ **Expert guidance**
An experienced, qualified trainer will be able to advise you and help solve any behaviour problems you may encounter with your puppy.

"Once your puppy learns how to play with toys and can do so **successfully,** he will **stop play biting."**

class size ensures you get more individual attention, and a trainer with a good knowledge of canine behaviour will be able to help you overcome any problems.

Surviving adolescence

Adolescence can be a difficult time, and all puppy owners need to prepare themselves for this phase. However, try not to worry – with the right attitude and perseverance, this period will soon be over and a lovely adult dog will emerge.

Exploring the world

Young puppies need us to care for them, and they work hard to keep our attention by being sweet and engaging. It is easy for us to enjoy this phase, but it does make it more difficult to accept the marked change in their attitude that occurs when they reach puberty at about six months. At this time, their focus naturally shifts to the outside world as all the hormones associated with reproduction begin to circulate. Suddenly, finding out about their environment and everything in it becomes their top priority, whereas previously their focus had been on pleasing us. Now that your puppy is bigger, stronger, and becoming more independent, you are less important to him than exploration, and he will probably begin to actively ignore you in favour of things outside.

Difficult time

This can be an awkward time for owners unless they are prepared for it. All their hard work seems to have been for nothing as their dog becomes rebellious, disinterested,

△ **Losing interest**
Unlike puppies, adolescent dogs are focused on the outside world and all it contains and are only occasionally interested in their owners.

and disobedient. Fortunately, adolescence is a passing phase that comes to a natural end. Dogs usually begin to mature at about one year, although some of the larger breeds do not reach full social maturity until they are around three years old. If you can ride out the difficulties that adolescence presents, your dog will eventually return to being the loving, attentive pet you once knew.

Not coming back

During adolescence, one of the most common problems for owners is their dogs not coming back when called on walks. The adolescent dog has other things to do, such as exploring, sniffing to find out who

◁ **Irresistible**
With their big eyes, short faces, and desire to please their owners, young puppies make us want to care for them and meet their needs.

and what has been in his territory, marking it with his own scent, and interacting with other dogs. During this time, he has the vigour and energy of an adult, but lacks the knowledge and experience that an older dog needs to stay out of trouble. Even if you had a good recall before, keep your dog on a long line in places where he may be tempted to go off without you, to prevent him getting into difficulties.

△ **The teenage phase**
Just as with humans, adolescence is a normal, natural process with accompanying behaviour changes that last until maturity is reached.

Trouble with other dogs

Adolescent dogs may also get into trouble as they get to know other dogs in the area and establish a ranking. If your dog begins to have aggressive encounters, keep away from unknown dogs and only allow interaction with friendly ones.

Don't give up

Many owners complain that during adolescence their dogs begin to be disobedient, no longer responding to commands. This is when some give up on their dogs and put them into rescue, which is unnecessary. Adolescence is just a phase and when the dogs mature, they will be willing to please again. Don't make too many requests that are unlikely to be met, but do gently insist that your dog does as you ask.

▽ **Keeping control**
During adolescence, it is advisable to use a long line when out on walks, to prevent your dog ignoring your recall cues or getting into trouble.

Elderly dogs

Just like humans, dogs gradually begin to slow down and their bodies start to fail as they get older. Understanding and adapting to their changing needs will help them to remain content and happy into old age.

The effects of ageing

There are big differences in how long dogs live. Giant dogs, such as the Great Dane, are lucky if they make it to nine years old, whereas Jack Russell Terriers sometimes live until they are 20. However, as a general rule, most dogs over 10 years old fall into the "elderly" category. After this age, their bodies are less suited to vigorous activity and will slowly decline as they get older. Along with the bodily changes that age brings, the mind also starts to run more slowly and tiredness takes over, with more and more time spent sleeping.

In addition, failing senses provide less information about their world. The eyes and ears are usually the first to fade, with the sense of smell outlasting all others. Cataracts may cloud the lenses of the eyes, making it more difficult to see, and some hearing ranges are lost, so sounds appear distorted or muffled. Since they can no longer be sure about their surroundings, elderly dogs may be likely to do things that are out of character. They may snap if touched

◁ **Happy old age**
Elderly dogs can live a contented life with owners who help them through the changes old age brings.

◁ **Do not disturb**
Elderly dogs need more rest, and you should provide a comfortable, warm, and safe place to sleep where they will not be disturbed.

unexpectedly because they cannot hear you approaching. Waking them gently by standing beside them long enough for them to smell you before you touch them can help prevent bitten fingers. Along with failing senses, painful joints cause stiffness and lack of mobility. This brings a reluctance to move, and can result in defensive biting if dogs think that they are about to be moved in a painful way, especially by children, who do not understand their condition.

△ **Failing senses**
An elderly dog may jump and even bite defensively when he is touched unexpectedly, because he did not notice someone approaching.

▷ **Old joints**
Stiff, painful joints may make old dogs reluctant to move. Veterinary advice, medication, and gentle exercise can help get them moving again.

Slowing down

To keep your dog living happily into old age, he must stay active and engaged with life. He will need more sleep than when he was younger, but noticing when he is awake and playing and encouraging him to take exercise and be part of the family are important. Don't forget him for long periods because he sleeps more. Adjust to his speed, so he feels comfortable, not rushed, and valued.

Problems with elderly dogs

Life with an elderly dog can be made easier if you deal successfully with some of the common problems that old age brings. With a little help and understanding, many difficulties can be overcome.

Car travel

Problems due to ageing bodies and minds are common in older dogs, but there is much you can do to make them to feel safe and content in their final years. For example, car journeys can become daunting for a dog who is already shaky on his feet. Finding a way to get him into the car without hurting him is important, whether this is by lifting him up or using a ramp. Once inside, providing a padded bed and taking corners and road bumps carefully can prevent him from losing his balance and having a painful fall.

Phobias and fears

Failing senses and reduced confidence late in life can lead to an elderly dog developing phobias and fears. Noises that he once tolerated, such as thunder, fireworks, and even rain on a roof, may suddenly become frightening to the elderly dog. Lots of understanding and patience are needed to avoid situations in which he feels threatened.

In addition to specific fears, old dogs may develop generalized fears, such as not being able to tolerate being left alone in the dark. If this is the case, reorganize his sleeping arrangements, so that he can sleep near to the family and feel safe. This usually solves the problem, but if it persists, your vet may be able to help with drugs and behaviour therapy.

Regular check-ups

Many of the behavioural changes and problems that occur in old age are caused by physical conditions, such as pain-induced behavioural changes produced by arthritis. It is vital to arrange regular check-ups for your dog with the vet. Changes due to ageing are often slow to

△ **How to lift**
If you are lifting an older dog, whether to get him into the car or for any other reason, take care not to squeeze him in such a way that you compress painful joints or limbs.

▷ **Car ramp**
Large, heavy dogs who can no longer jump and cannot be lifted may need a specially designed ramp to get into the car. This will enable them to walk slowly into the car with the minimum of discomfort.

"Failing senses and **reduced confidence** late in life **can result in** an elderly dog developing **phobias** and **fears."**

△ Minimize change
If your dog has failing sight, try to keep the furniture in the same place to help him find his way safely around your home. If changes are essential, make them one at a time.

appear, but regular examination by a vet will help identify signs or symptoms of treatable conditions.

Cognitive dysfunction syndrome

Similar to Alzheimer's Disease in humans, cognitive dysfunction syndrome can affect older dogs. Symptoms of the condition include:

■ Confusion or disorientation, such as getting lost or trapped in corners.
■ Waking at night or a change in sleeping patterns.
■ House-training difficulties.
■ Decreased attention span or staring into space.

△ Confused thinking
Old dogs can become confused. You may find that they get lost or try to get out of the door on the wrong side. Ask your vet if medication can help.

Routine is important

As dogs age and become fragile, routine becomes very important. Regular feeding, exercise, and toileting opportunities, together with a constant diet, will help to prevent loss of house-training and keep their bodies working well. Old dogs sleep a lot, and it is easy to forget they are there. A routine will help you remember to allow enough time to give your dog the love, play, and stimulation he needs.

■ Pacing or lack of usual activity.
■ Not recognizing family, and a decline in your shared relationship.
  Some symptoms may be part of the natural ageing process; others may be due to changes in the dog's brain that can be improved by medication.

▽ Tender loving care
Providing your old dog with extra care and understanding can lead to a quality of life that will bring him contentment for many years.

3

Basic
training

How dogs learn

To be a successful trainer, you must **understand how the learning process works in dogs.** With this knowledge, all practical training tasks will be easier for both you and your dog. This section tells you **all you need to know to train successfully,** and explains how to **get your dog to do what you want,** so you can **reward the action.** It also offers advice on **which rewards to use,** when to begin to phase them out, and what to replace them with. Find out why **timing is critical to successful training,** and how dogs learn sets of **associations,** as well as how bad habits can be unlearned almost as easily as they were learned in the first place.

POSITIVE TRAINING
Dogs learn very quickly if it is in their best interest to do so. Reward-based training is fun for both dog and owner.

Trial, error, and success

Understanding how dogs learn is essential if we are to teach them how to respond to our requests easily and with minimal confusion. It will also cut down the time it takes to train them.

The learning process

Dogs learn by trial, error, and success, just like humans. They will repeat any action that leads to a successful outcome, and will avoid those actions that go unrewarded or have unpleasant consequences. For example, a dog who burns his nose on a hot stove will not wish to do so again. Likewise, a puppy who barks for attention and is ignored will

◁ **Learning**
The smell of food inside a flip-top bin encourages this dog to use his initiative to find a way to get at it. Once he learns how, he will be able to repeat this task with ease.

cease to do it. However, a dog who jumps up to greet his owner and is rewarded with fuss and attention will repeat this action, and it will soon become a bad habit that is very difficult to break (pp.188–9).

Learning to respond

We can use our dogs' ability to learn from their actions by rewarding the behaviours we want to be repeated,

△ **Get the action**
To teach a puppy to respond to a request, you need to find a way to get him to do the action you require.

△ **Respond on cue**
Once the puppy has learned what you want him to do, this action can be put on cue, so you can ask him to do it again.

The three-minute rule

Our dogs lie around most of the time with their brains in neutral. Asking them to think and work out what we require during training is tiring for them, so always make training sessions less than three minutes long. Set a timer, as it is easy to get carried away and to keep on training until you are both tired and frustrated. Instead, keep each session short and end on a positive note with a successful outcome. Go back to something easier if necessary, so that you both look forward to the next session.

◁ **Trial and error**
Since he lacks a sophisticated brain to figure out this problem, the dog needs to keep trying different actions until one of them is successful.

and ignoring or preventing those we dislike. We can also utilize this technique when we want to train our dogs to respond to our requests, such as to come when called (pp.124–5) or to lie down (pp.126–7). To train a dog to do something for us, all we need to do is get him to perform the action and then reward it, so that he does it again next time.

△ **Success!**
This dog may have succeeded, but he needs to repeat this action several times before he learns what he must do to get the stick through the gate.

Since dogs do not understand what we are saying (although sometimes people think they do, as they are so good as reading our non-verbal language), we cannot tell them with words what we want them to do. Instead, we need to cleverly arrange

for them to do the action we require (p.110) and then reward them. Once this is going well and they know how to get the rewards in that situation, we can put the action on cue by giving a voice cue or hand signal just before we arrange for them to carry out the action.

A training example

If you want your dog to lie down when you ask, first lure him into position using a carefully held edible treat (p.110). As soon as his elbows reach the floor, feed him the treat. Repeat this exercise until he knows what to do in order to get the treat. Then put the action on cue by giving a hand signal or the voice cue "down" (pp.110–11) just before you lure him into position. After many repetitions of this action, he will learn that when you give a certain signal he will be rewarded if he lies down, and he will begin to do so whenever asked. Train him to do this in a variety of situations (pp.114–5). When he has learned how to respond to the cue, you will be able to reduce the rewards you offer (pp.116–7).

Rewards

Rewards are essential to the success of positive training techniques. Knowing how to use them and what your dog will find most rewarding will make training him easy and more enjoyable for both of you.

108

Types of reward

To teach your dog to do something, you need to reward him as soon as he performs the required action with something he really wants. What you use depends on your dog, and the options are listed below.

Food This is easy to use as it can be fed and eaten relatively quickly to reward the required action. Food that is used in training needs to be:

■ Appetizing – meat appeals to dogs more than anything else.

■ Smelly – dogs have quite a poor sense of taste compared to smell.

■ Moist – moist food is usually more appetizing than dry food.

■ Soft – it needs to be easy to break up into small pieces.

■ Easy to handle – so that you do not have to wait while your dog cleans up the pieces you drop on the floor.

■ The right size – offer little pieces, about the size of a small pea, for small dogs, or a large pea for larger dogs. These are sufficient to reward an easy task. Use slightly larger pieces or food of a higher value for the more difficult tasks (see below).

Games These can be very useful if your dog is playful, but has a poor appetite. Compared with using food, it takes longer to reward him, because he has to play a short game and then you have to get the toy back from him afterwards. However, for some dogs who enjoy

△ **Small rewards**
Dogs will work hard for small pieces of food if they are sufficiently appetizing. Use a treat bag to help prevent a sticky mess in your pocket.

Hierarchy of rewards

Find out what your dog likes and grade them from most liked to least favourite. Use the lowest-value rewards for easy tasks, such as sitting (pp.122–3), and the highest-value ones for difficult exercises, for example coming back when playing with another dog (pp.148–9). What your dog views as high value will change over time, so keep checking what he likes most. Dogs get bored easily, and varying what is on offer will help to keep your dog's performance levels high.

Training treats

Cheese cubes

Meaty strips

Frankfurter pieces

Moist treats

Cooked chicken

Cooked sausage

△ **Social approval**
Really make a connection with your dog when giving him social approval, as this will mean a lot more to him than just a quick pat on the head.

play, games are powerful motivators and they can be utilized in addition to food as a high-value reward for a very difficult task.

Social approval

Social approval, in the form of praise, affection, and social contact, is a very powerful reward for social animals, especially if you have a good relationship with your dog (pp.66–7). Since our pet dogs are usually not starved of this kind of attention, social approval has a limited use by itself, but it is still a useful addition to providing food and games as rewards for your dog. This is especially true when the time comes to reduce the quantity of rewards given (pp.116–7).

△ **Playing with toys**
Games with toys make a good and enjoyable reward for dogs who know how to play. They are also useful for those with small appetites or who are not interested in traditional food treats.

> "Find out **what your dog likes,** then **grade** them from **most liked to least favourite.**"

Wanting the reward

Judging what your dog wants at any moment in time and offering it for successful compliance is key to success. Just as you may crave different things at different times of the day or week, so it is for your dog. Ensure he is peckish before training him with food, and that he is active and ready to play if you are using toys. If he is not interested in training, try to work out what would interest and motivate him more.

Make it happen

We cannot explain to our dogs what we want them to do, so we need to find other means of getting them to do the actions we require. There are a variety of ways in which you can get your dog to carry out certain actions.

Getting the action

To achieve certain actions, try the following methods:

Luring You can lure your dog into position by holding an appetizing morsel of food against his nose and moving it slowly in the direction you want him to go. The piece of food needs to be big enough for the dog to lick and chew at, so you can keep him interested while you move it. Where his nose goes, his head and body will follow.

As soon as you get your dog into position, feed the treat as a reward, so he learns that going into that position brings a good result. This increases the likelihood of him doing it again more easily next time. Luring is particularly useful for inexperienced puppies and dogs.

Shaping If you reward your dog for making any movement that takes him in the direction you want him to go, he will learn, eventually, to go in that direction to get the reward. You are shaping his behaviour by rewarding him initially for making small movements towards your desired goal, then gradually allowing him to move closer to the goal before rewarding him.

This method is useful for more experienced dogs who know that you want them to do something and try different actions to find out what it is. It is similar to the game of "Hot and Cold" played by children.

△ **Learning from others**
Dogs may join in with natural behaviour, such as barking at strangers, but they find it difficult to learn complex tasks by mimicry.

◁ **Follow the treat**
Luring is an easy way to get a novice dog to move into different positions so that you can reward the action.

Targeting If you teach your dog over several sessions to touch a target with either his nose or paw, you can then move the target to get him to move to different locations. Try using this technique if you want your dog to do something that is not a natural behaviour, such as turning off a light or pressing a pedal.

Mimicry Dogs find it difficult to mimic the behaviour of other animals, so this technique is not very effective for training purposes. Dogs will learn by joining in with natural behaviours, such as barking

△ **Target training**
Targeting is used to get dogs to do things they would not do naturally. This dog is learning how to close a cupboard door with his nose.

at strangers, but they find it difficult to learn complicated tasks from others in this way.

Modelling A common way to make a dog sit is to push down on his hindquarters. However, not only is this dangerous for puppies or fragile dogs with growing or weak joints, but it also causes a resistance as the dog pushes up against the pressure. Any resistance means that he takes longer to learn what you want of him.

Hand signals

Once your dog can do the required action, you need to put it on cue. Hand signals should be given just before the action (pp.112–3) so that your dog can make the connection. After enough repetition, your dog will perform the action when you give the hand signal.

SIT
This hand signal is an upward motion with a flat hand. Begin with an exaggerated movement that starts near your thigh and ends at your shoulder. Make sure the palm is facing up. Once your dog knows this, reduce the movement gradually.
》122–3

COME
This signal consists of a movement of the arms held alongside the body and then brought out from the body to the position shown here. When you first begin training this exercise, you will be crouching, so the movement is made with the hands together, and then the arms are taken out to either side.
》124–5

WAIT
To make this signal, hold your hand flat, then bring it down slowly towards your dog's face and hold it stationary. Try to position your hand so that your dog can still see your face; otherwise, he may move in order to try to see around it.
》128–9

DOWN
This hand signal consists of a downward motion with a flat hand. Begin with an exaggerated movement that starts near your shoulder and ends at the thigh. The palm should be facing down. Once your dog knows this, reduce the movement slowly.
》126–7

WALK CLOSE
The signal for "walk close" is made by holding your hand on your hip. Because movements are more effective as signals, you can pat your side initially so that your dog moves closer to investigate your hand before rewarding him. Eventually, you will no longer need to move your hand to give the signal.
》132–3

STAND
For the "stand" hand signal, hold a flat hand in front of your dog's nose and then draw it away. This action is very similar to the luring action and your dog should learn it easily. Reduce the signal gradually once your dog learns what you require.
》130–1

Timing

Timing is really important to successful training. Good timing speeds up the training process and aids communication with your dog so that he can easily understand what you require of him.

Speed is essential

Delivering a reward as soon as your dog has done the required action is the only way you have to tell him he has done what you wanted him to do. Remember that actions that are rewarded are likely to be repeated. Since you want your chosen action to be repeated, and not the action that follows it (e.g. the sit rather than the getting up), you need to be quick so that you reward at a time when your dog is still thinking about the sit rather than about getting up to move on.

Instant reward

Watch your dog closely while you encourage the correct action. Learn to anticipate when he will go into position or do the correct action

△ **Reward immediately**
When teaching your dog to sit, watch him carefully and reward him just as his bottom touches the floor. This will let him know exactly what is required next time.

▷ **Be prepared**
Taking more than two seconds to give the reward means that your dog will have moved on to thinking about something else instead of what you wanted to reward.

Hand signal and voice cue | **Action** | **Positive reinforcement**

and have the reward ready. You need to deliver rewards instantly, so keep food and toys close and begin to reach for them as soon as your dog begins to do the action. Be careful, however. If you hold rewards where a dog can see them while he is thinking about what to do, they will only distract rather than encourage him, so keep them out of sight – unless, of course, you are using them as a lure.

Once your dog has performed the desired action, you must reward him immediately, so have

moved on to thinking about something else, you will be rewarding this action instead and your dog will not learn what you want him to do. He will be confused about what you want or will respond in a way that is different to what you expected, and training will be a confusing, frustrating experience for you both.

Timing cues
To put an action on cue – in other words, to teach your dog to respond to a signal such as the command

△ **Timing is crucial**
The voice cue and hand signal should be given first. Then lure your dog into position if he does not understand the cue or signal. As soon as he has done the required action, reward instantly. After many repetitions, leave a gap of a few moments between the cue/signal and the action, to see if your dog understands what to do.

begin to respond as soon as he sees or hears the cue, rather than waiting for the lure or whatever else you are using to gain the desired response.

> **"Learn to anticipate** when he will go into **position** or do the **correct action** and have the **reward ready."**

everything in place. For example, try keeping a reward concealed in your hand, but keep it well away from your dog's nose – otherwise, the smell will take his attention away from training. If you are too late and reward after your dog has

word "sit" or a hand pointing to the ground (see above) – give the cue just before you make the action happen. Repeated use of the cue will allow your dog to associate the cue with the desired action. Eventually he will

Steps to learning cues
When you teach a new action, first use a lure or other encouragement over several sessions until your dog can do it easily. Then add the voice cue and hand signals over several sessions so he begins to make the connection. Later, add a short gap of a few counts between the cue and making the action happen to give your dog time to work out what you want. At first, reward any small movement towards what you want. Later, wait for the complete action before rewarding.

Associations

Dogs learn a set of associations when we teach them to respond to a cue such as "sit". For the cue to work anywhere, we need to teach it to our dogs in a variety of different situations.

Responding to cues

When a dog is being taught to respond to a cue, he is learning to associate a hand signal or word with a particular action. By repetition over several training sessions, he will learn to carry out the action whenever he sees or hears the cue.

Be aware that as well as learning the cue, your dog is learning a set of associations surrounding the event. When we teach a puppy to sit for his dinner, we may think he has learned the word "sit". What he has actually learned is that when he is standing in front of you in the kitchen and you hold his dish in your hand, all he needs to do to get you to place the dish on the floor is to put his bottom on the ground when you say "sit". Remove

Learning word cues

The only cue that most pet dogs learn is "sit". This is because it is repeated over and over by owners in many different situations in their everyday lives until their dogs know it well. However, dogs are capable of learning hundreds of words, provided that they are carefully taught. If you want your dog to understand all the major control cues, such as "come", "down", "stay", and "heel", you need to work hard and consistently to teach him each of these in turn in many different situations and circumstances.

▽ **Learned associations**
This puppy has learned that he will get his food if he puts his bottom on the floor when facing his owner as she holds the dish.

any of these associations, and the puppy will not understand what you want and will remain standing.

To overcome this, teach your dog the same lesson in many different situations. As the cue is the only association that these experiences have in common, he will eventually learn to link the cue with the correct action to win his reward.

You also need to teach your dog the same lesson in many different positions relative to you. Otherwise, if you teach him to sit in front of you, and then ask him to do it when he is beside you, he will move round to sit in front of you, where he was previously rewarded. By varying your position relative to him during training, he will learn that there is a reward for responding to the cue wherever he is.

All this takes a long time, so be patient. Never punish your dog for not obeying you – he simply does not understand. Instead, show him what is required, and make sure you reward him well for doing it.

△ **Practise in different places**
This puppy is learning to sit on cue when standing in front of his owner in the garden – a different location to where he previously learned to carry out this action.

▷ **Sitting on cue**
Here the puppy is learning that he will be rewarded for sitting when his owner is sitting in a chair. After many training sessions, he will begin to understand what the cue "sit" means.

Random rewards

It is unnecessary to continuously use food as a reward once your dog has learned what to do. Weaning him onto occasional reinforcements and "jackpots" improves performance and reduces his reliance on treats.

Do not reward every time

When your dog understands completely what you require him to do when you give a particular hand signal or voice cue, you can begin reducing the number of rewards you offer. This needs to be done very gradually, until eventually you are rewarding about one in every five responses at random. This can be hard to do initially, but to help keep rewards random, try putting five buttons in your pocket, one of which is a different colour, and reward your dog only when you pull out the coloured one. When you decide not to reward a response to a cue, always tell him he is correct (see box), letting him know that he has done the right thing by giving him lots of praise.

Jackpots

It has been shown that reducing rewards in this way causes animals

> "**Jackpots** do not need to happen very often, but most **dogs will work really hard** to earn them if they **appear at random.**"

116

◁ **Boost incentive**
Giving occasional rewards and jackpots can really improve performance because most dogs, like the one shown here, will try hard to "win" more treats more often.

△ **Expectations**
Lack of reward can cause confusion at first, as your dog will expect a reward every time he performs the correct action, but he will soon learn the new regime.

▷ **The pay-off**
A jackpot is a time for celebrating. The more fun your dog has, the more he will remember the jackpot and the harder he will work for it next time.

to work harder and for longer to earn treats. The effect becomes even more pronounced if you offer occasional "jackpots". These are something special your dog really likes, such as a handful of favourite treats together with lots of fuss and a game. Really make an occasion out of the "win" and celebrate with your dog for maximum effect.

If you do this, you will find that he begins to "gamble" on the outcome in the same way you do when buying a lottery ticket: sometimes you get nothing, but there is a chance that you will win a small prize or, better still, the jackpot. Jackpots do not need to happen very often, but dogs will work really hard to earn them if they appear at random. If you save them for excellent performances, overall performance will improve.

You may think it is unfair to reward some responses and not others, so it is your choice whether to try this or not. Some dogs are highly competitive, whereas others will give up more easily. However, for many dogs, random rewards are an effective way of improving their performance.

◁ **Give him credit**
Always reward difficult actions and hard decisions, such as when your dog leaves his canine friends to come when you call him.

How dogs learn

Good dog

To make it easier for your dog to know that he has done something correctly, practise a word or phrase you can say as soon as he does the required action, such as "good dog". Make sure you reward him with treats soon afterwards. Over the course of many training sessions, this word or phrase will become linked to the reward, and can be used to let the dog know that he has done the right thing. When you move on to occasional rewards, use this signal to let him know he has done what you require, even when you do not reward him.

△ **Reward every time**
When training a new exercise, offer a reward every time your dog is successful, until he knows exactly what is expected when he is given a particular cue.

Reward rules

The rules for giving reinforcement rewards and jackpots are as follows:
- Only use them when the dog really understands what you want him to do. Failure to reward an action before it is completely learned will lead to confusion.
- Make sure your dog enjoys his "wins". Really celebrate a "jackpot".

- Let your dog know he was correct and praise him well each time, whether or not you give a reward.
- Always reward difficult actions or complicated sequences of behaviour.

Reversing bad habits

Dogs can learn bad habits if they are rewarded unwittingly for unwanted behaviour, but they can be unlearned just as easily provided that their owners know what to do and work hard to change their pets' behaviour.

Curing bad habits

Dogs can unlearn a "bad" behaviour if you are able to remove the reward they receive when they do it. This is useful for dealing with behaviours that owners reward unwittingly, such as jumping up (pp.188–9) or

△ **Getting comfortable**
For some laid-back owners, relaxing on the sofa is a perfectly acceptable behaviour for their dog, but others would prefer that he slept elsewhere.

giving their dogs attention when they are performing unwanted actions. Before you attempt this, however, you should make sure that your dog is getting everything he needs in order to feel content. This may seem obvious, but taking a look at life from your dog's point of view can often reveal inadequacies in his care that his bad behaviour is actually trying to address.

To cure your dog's bad habit, the whole family must work together in ignoring the unwanted behaviour. This can be difficult, especially if your dog is barking excessively, in which case warn your neighbours and buy some ear plugs. It is really important that you do completely ignore the barking, which means not speaking to your dog, looking at him, or touching him. Just look

the other way, then turn away and pretend that you are not interested. Do not reprimand your dog – for some dogs, even being told off is better than being ignored. If the behaviour is self-rewarding, such as getting up on a comfortable sofa to sleep, you will need to stop or prevent it from happening while you encourage an alternative, equally rewarding behaviour.

Worse behaviour

For a short time, it is likely that your dog's behaviour will get worse instead of better, so be prepared for this. When the behaviour that has worked so well for him in the past is no longer working, he will try even harder to get what he wants. He will also feel frustrated, which, in turn, will make his behaviour worse.

△ **Get down**
If your dog has settled down and made himself comfortable, he has already been rewarded for sitting on the sofa and is more likely to do it again.

△ **No reward**
Attach a long line to your dog's collar to prevent him settling down every time he gets on the sofa, so he learns he is not rewarded by this action.

△ **Act quickly**
Ensure that you get him off the sofa before he gets comfortable. This means constant vigilance on your part until he has learned new habits.

However, if you continue to ignore him, eventually he will realize that this behaviour no longer works. It is very important to remember that any form of bad behaviour that goes unrewarded will cease, although it may take some time. Be patient and wait for this to happen.

To speed up the process, reward the behaviours you do want instead, such as being quiet or not jumping up. Once your dog realizes how to get rewarded for good behaviour, his "bad" behaviour, which is no longer being rewarded, will stop.

Occasional lapses

In spite of all this training, you must be prepared for occasional lapses as your dog will not forget those behaviours that have been

"For a short time, your dog's **behaviour** is **likely** to get **worse** instead of **better**."

rewarded, especially if they were rewarded often over a long period of time. Just continue to ignore them and you will find that they will subside. Try not to reward unwanted behaviour unwittingly, such as by telling him off when he is muddy and tries to jump up. Telling him off sometimes and ignoring him at other times will randomly reward him (pp.116–7); he will then try even harder to make the unwanted behaviour work.

△ **A good alternative**
Providing your dog with a comfortable place to lie down, which is suitable from his point of view, will quickly get him into good habits.

Prevention over cure

Since behaviours that are rewarded are remembered easily, especially during puppyhood, it is better if they are never learned at all. If you prevent a puppy from practising a behaviour until he is a year old, it is likely he will never think of doing it. If he is never encouraged onto a sofa or bed when young, he will get into the habit of going to his bed to sleep. If everyone bends down to greet him and prevents him jumping up on visitors, he will learn to stay on all four paws.

Good grounding

A well-trained dog is a real **pleasure to live with,** and can be included in your everyday activities instead of being left at home. He will be **easier to manage,** leaving you **more time for play and other fun-filled activities** that make dog ownership such a joy. Teaching your dog the **simple exercises** shown in this section will give you a way to **communicate** your wishes to your dog and allow you to **control his actions.** These exercises will also lay the foundations for the **more complex training** outlined in later sections, which will **advance his education** and allow you to teach him **useful skills, interesting tricks, and sports.**

HAPPY HEELWORK
Positive training using praise, rewards, and treats results in a dog that enjoys training sessions and tries really hard to please you.

Sit

Sit is one of the easiest exercises to teach and a very good place to start training your dog. It is the exercise that most owners teach first and the cue that is repeated most often throughout a dog's life.

A dog that is sitting is not jumping up, running off, barging through doorways, or misbehaving in any other way. Teaching your dog to sit gives you control and allows you to keep him in one place.

In addition, sitting quickly becomes the posture that most dogs adopt if they see that their owner has something they want, because they have been rewarded most often in this position.

1 △
Get his attention
With your dog standing, hold a tasty treat in your fingers and allow him to lick a small piece of it. Then slowly raise the treat and lure his nose steadily upwards.

2 ▷
Raise the treat
Move the treat gradually over your dog's head, giving him time to follow it up and backwards with his nose. Wait for his back legs to begin folding naturally.

GOOD PRACTICE

Once your dog can easily be lured into the sit position, give the voice cue "sit" just before you start. Continue to do so as you teach him to respond to a hand signal (right). After a number of sessions, once your dog is readily responding to the hand signal, you can begin to phase it out by making it less exaggerated.

If you always precede the hand signal and lure with the word "sit", your dog will eventually learn to respond to the voice cue alone.

Don't forget to train the sit exercise in different places, with your dog in different positions in relation to you (pp.114–5), and with increasing distractions going on all around.

Hand signal
Once your dog can easily be lured into the sit, teach him to respond to a hand signal. Get his attention, give a clear hand signal, wait a moment, then lure your dog into a sit as before.

If you are struggling to keep your dog focused during training sessions, increase the value of the treat you are offering (pp.206–7) to keep him interested for longer.

It is important to hold the treat in the right place when teaching this exercise. Take care not to hold it too high above your dog's nose or too far back.

Jumping up
If your dog has to jump up in order to reach the treat, lower your hand so that he can reach it throughout the luring process.

3 △

Reward
As soon as your dog's rear end touches the floor, give him the treat and praise him enthusiastically. Feed him two or three more treats while he remains sitting.

Come when called

Come when called is an essential lesson. It will allow you to let your dog safely off his lead, confident that you can recall him if you need to, and enable you to give him more exercise and freedom.

The early stages of the come when called exercise, shown here, are easy. Once your dog has learned these, you can build up reliable recalls outside the home as well (pp.146–9). Having a dog that comes to you when called makes life easier in both home and garden. Knowing that you can recall him even from a distance will give you peace of mind and make walks safer and more enjoyable for you both.

1 △
Tempt him
Start this exercise somewhere familiar to your dog. Ask a friend to hold your dog's collar while you show him an enticing training treat and allow him to sniff at it.

2 ▷
"Come!"
Move a short distance (about 2m/6ft) away and crouch down at your dog's level with your arms open wide. Call him enthusiastically, encouraging him to come towards you.

3.
Lure him in
As your dog reaches you, having responded to your call, hold out the treat so that he can see it, and lure him towards you.

"Always **make the reward worthwhile** for your dog."

5.
"Well done!"
When your dog reaches you, keep holding his collar as you feed him the treat. Praise him warmly, so that he learns to enjoy being with you and will come again when he is called.

4.
Take his collar
Holding the treat at his nose-height, lure him closer. Hold the other hand lower, so you can gently take hold of his collar under his chin.

GOOD PRACTICE

When practising this exercise, call your dog only when there is a good chance he will respond immediately. This will encourage good habits. If your dog does not come to you, try using a more interesting treat (p.106).

If he is shy, turn sideways when you call and avoid direct eye contact, so that you don't intimidate him.

Don't call too often once your dog knows what to do; call him only when you have something worthwhile to offer him.

Never tell your dog off for coming to you when you've called, even if he does not come to you immediately.

Keep your call consistent in tone and volume, even when you call in an emergency. He may not recognize a louder or deeper call.

"Come" body signal
Dogs learn body signals easily. They are useful if your dog is far away and cannot hear you. Slowly progress from crouching (opposite) to standing.

Down

Teaching your dog to lie down on request makes living with him easier, and allows you to control him in a variety of situations. It is a more stable position than the sit when attempting to keep him still.

Down is a building block of basic training and allows you to teach advanced exercises such as settle (pp.192–3) and down at a distance (pp.152–3).

It is easy to teach, but you will need patience at first to lure your dog into the right position. Reward him as often for lying down on request as you reward him for sitting and he will do both with equal ease.

1 △
Get his attention
Find a quiet, familiar location to teach this exercise. With your dog sitting (pp.122–3), lure his head slowly downwards using a treat. Allow him to lick and chew a small piece of the treat so he stays focused.

2 ▷
Lure him down
Keep moving the treat slowly downwards. If your dog loses concentration, start the process again and feed him the treat just before you reach the point where he gave up previously. Replace that treat with another and try again immediately.

GOOD PRACTICE

When first teaching the "down" hand signal (pp.110–11), make an exaggerated hand movement, bringing the hand with the food in it all the way to the floor so that your dog can follow it.

Be aware that the down position can make your dog feel more vulnerable in any situation that makes him insecure, such as in places where other dogs are present.

Hand signal
Once he responds to being lured, teach your dog to lie down using a hand signal. Get his attention, give a clear hand signal, then wait a few seconds before luring him down as above.

When your dog has learned the hand signal for down, teach him to respond to a voice command. Give the command "down" just before you start, then give your hand signal. Eventually, he will lie down when he hears the word "down".

Once he has learned this exercise, teach your dog to lie down in different places, in various positions in relation to you (pp.114–5). Eventually, he will do so in the midst of a wide range of distractions.

3 ◁
Reward

As soon as your dog's elbows touch the ground, feed him the treat. Praise him warmly and reward him with an extra treat while he remains in the down position to let him know that this is what you wanted him to do.

"**Only ask** your dog to lie down in **environments** where he **feels safe and secure.**"

Try again
If your dog stands, ask him to sit again, then hold the treat further away from him so that he has room to lie down without going backwards.

Under the bridge
If you are struggling to teach the down position, make a bridge with your legs and lure your dog through. He will have to lie down to earn his treat.

Avoid discomfort
Dogs with deep, narrow chests or sparse belly fur may find it uncomfortable to lie on hard floors – try using a thick, squashy bed instead.

Wait

Wait is a simple exercise to teach, and will make it easy for you to keep your dog in one position while you do something else, such as put his food down on the floor or open the door to go out.

Teach your dog to wait only when he has learned to sit reliably (pp.122–3). It is not a very interesting exercise for your dog to learn as he has nothing to do, so make sure he is tired and therefore happy to rest in one position when you start teaching. Once you have taught him that all he needs to do to get his reward is stay in one place, you can begin to teach him to do so while you move around him.

1 ◁
Sit, then wait
Ask your dog to sit. When he is sitting and you have his attention, say "wait", and give your hand signal for wait. If he moves, try again, but move your hand more slowly as you give the signal. A hand signal given quickly may cause him to move.

2 ▽
Reward
Reward him well with two or three treats while he stays in place. Practise this until he waits reliably, then leave a short gap before rewarding him. Continue over several sessions, extending the gap until he will wait for up to two minutes.

> **"Never leave** your dog in the **wait position** in a **potentially dangerous place."**

3. ▽ Step slowly back

Give your voice cue and hand signal, then step one foot backwards. Slowly transfer your weight onto that foot, then return and reward your dog. If he moves, reposition him and repeat, but step away more slowly.

4. ▷ Circle your dog

Continue over several sessions, gradually moving further away from your dog. Take care when moving behind him as dogs often get up when they can no longer follow you easily with their eyes.

5. △ Distance work

Over several sessions, when your dog understands what he has to do, you will be able to move even further away. Always return to reward him during training, so he knows he has to stay on that spot to receive his treats.

GOOD PRACTICE

Once your dog understands what you want him to do, you can ask him to wait in practical situations, for example at a doorway (pp.194–5). On release, he will have something exciting to do, such as running out of the door. Always reward him well in "wait" before you release him. Otherwise, his wait will become unreliable as he begins to anticipate the reward associated with being released.

Hand signal
Wait is one of the only exercises where you teach the hand signal from the start. Keep your hand signals slow and calm during early training.

Stay down
You can also teach this exercise with your dog in the down position (pp.126–7). Down is often a more settled position.

Stand

Teaching your dog to stand when asked is useful for getting him into position if you need to towel him dry. Having a dog that will stand patiently is also invaluable on visits to the vets.

The stand position is useful if you are planning to show your dog, and it has many practical applications too, such when you want to put a harness on your dog or wipe his muddy feet. Before you begin training your dog to stand following the stages shown here, he needs to know how to sit when you ask (pp.122–3).

Present a treat
With your dog in the sit position, place a tasty treat against his nose so he can lick and nibble it, and then start to move it away slowly.

Lure him towards you
As your dog moves his head forwards to try to get to the treat, keep it moving slowly away from him until he has to get up to reach it.

GOOD PRACTICE

Move the treat just enough to make your dog stand up to get it, but bring the treat back to him quickly once he has done so to prevent him moving forwards.

Give the voice cue "stand" just before you lure your dog into the stand. When your dog has learned the hand signal, leave a gap between the voice cue and the hand signal to give him time to respond to the voice cue alone.

Hand signal
Once your dog has learned the stand, develop the luring action into a hand signal, using an exaggerated movement. Reduce this movement over several sessions (pp.110–11).

Don't forget to practise the stand exercise in different places, with your dog in different positions in relation to you (pp.114–5) and, eventually, with distractions going on all around.

Show dogs are required to stand still for long periods. If you own a show dog, make "stand" the default position by requesting it when most owners would ask their dog to sit. Gradually lengthen the time he stands before rewarding him, so he learns to hold the position.

3

Praise him

As soon as he stands, and before he steps forward, feed him the treat and praise him effusively. Practise over several sessions, gradually flattening your palm and building the lure into a hand signal (below left).

Walking on a **loose lead 1**

This is one of the most difficult exercises to teach, but it is so rewarding when your dog learns to walk happily beside you on a loose lead. You need lots of patience to achieve this, following and practising the steps shown here and on pp.134–5.

Taking regular walks with your dog is important for both the mental and physical well-being of your dog, and provides health benefits for you as well. Teach this skill as early in your dog's life as possible, as a dog that is comfortable walking next to you on a loose lead is a pleasure to walk. Once you have taught this exercise, practise in a variety of locations, with increasing distractions. Then teach him not to pull on the lead (pp.134–5), but to walk nicely wherever he is.

> "Gradually **extend the number of paces you take** each time."

2 ▽

"Heel"
Show your dog another treat and raise it above his head – hold it so he can see it clearly. Get his attention by saying his name and give the voice cue "heel".

1 △

Position him
Hold the lead in your right hand, and against your body. Hold a tasty treat in your other hand and lure your dog into position alongside your left leg, feeding the treat when your dog is in place.

GOOD PRACTICE

At the beginning of each training session and whenever you are in a new area, reward your dog after only taking one pace until your dog learns what to do.

Once your dog is walking beside you, show the hand signal (right) just before you set off. If he moves out of position, stand still and lure him back into place before taking a step forward.

Hand signal
Teach your dog to respond to a hand signal (pp.110–1). A flat palm positioned at your hip is a clear signal for your dog to stay close.

During training, choose which side of you your dog should walk and stick to it to avoid confusion. Once your dog knows what is expected, you can train him to walk on the other side of you if required.

It is difficult, at first, to coordinate the lead, treats, and dog. Stop and reposition your dog as necessary, rewarding him when he is in the correct position. Only move forward when ready, and praise well when your dog walks close.

4
Practise
Continue in this way, over several sessions, gradually extending the number of paces you take each time before rewarding him.

3 △
Step forwards and reward
Immediately take a pace forward and, as your dog follows, reward him with the treat and lots of praise. Repeat, rewarding after two paces, then three, and so on.

Lead length
The lead should hang down slightly from your dog's collar when standing next to you with the handle held at your waist, but not touch the floor.

No jumping
If your dog jumps up to get the treat while you are walking, raise the treat higher and keep walking until he stops jumping, then reward him.

Mind over matter
Try not to use the lead to control your dog, and keep the food lure in the hand nearest to your dog so he doesn't try to walk in front of you.

Walking on a **loose lead 2**

Training your dog not to pull is a vital part of learning to walk on a loose lead. Before teaching this exercise, ensure that your dog has learned how to walk next to you, and does so easily (pp.132–3).

Whenever you take your dog to a new and exciting place, she is likely to be distracted by the unfamiliar sights and smells around her. Before you can teach her that pulling on the lead is unacceptable in any

surroundings, it is essential that she has learned that she has to walk close to you on a loose lead instead (pp.132–3). Start this exercise by walking normally with your dog on a loose lead beside you.

1 △
Walk normally
Walk normally until your dog begins to pull ahead. Keep the lead-holding hand held into your middle to give a fixed length of lead.

2 ▽
Stop abruptly
Watch the lead carefully and stop abruptly when the lead begins to go tight. Keep your hands against your body and resist the pull from your dog.

3 △
Lure her back into position
Stand still and use a treat to get your dog's attention. Lure her back into the correct position by your side, facing forwards. When she is in the right place, reward her with the treat and praise enthusiastically.

4
Be alert
Watch out for distractions that may cause your dog to pull, such as other dogs, and stop as necessary. If you stop abruptly and reposition every time the lead goes tight, your dog will learn that pulling is not rewarding.

5
Relax and enjoy
Keep practising this exercise until your dog has learned not to pull. If she forgets and pulls forwards, stop and reposition her immediately. Reward her when she makes an effort to keep the lead loose. You can then relax your hands and give her more freedom.

GOOD PRACTICE

Teaching your dog not to pull on the lead when out walking takes time and patience, especially if she has been pulling for some time. Be consistent with your training and expect to stop as many as 40 times during your first walk. You will need to stop less frequently as she learns that pulling is not rewarding.

Too much energy
It is easier to teach a well-exercised dog to walk on a loose lead. Take your dog for a run or play games before training to use up excess energy.

Good practice
When teaching this exercise, allow extra time for walks so you can practise. If you don't have time, use a head collar (shown here) or harness.

Retrieve 1

Once your dog has learned to play, teaching him to retrieve items on demand will ensure that he spends more time running after an object than you do. The first step is to encourage enthusiasm for a favourite toy.

The key to helping your dog learn the retrieve is to create a sense of enthusiasm and excitement for a favourite toy. Once he has learned to chase and pick up a toy, you can progress to asking him to bring it back to you (pp.138–9). Follow the steps below, practising over several sessions until your dog shows instant enthusiasm for running out and picking up the toy whenever it is thrown.

1 △
Creating excitement
Begin by playing with one of your dog's favourite toys. Have fun, and be as enthusiastic as possible to drum up his excitement. Keep the toy moving and tease him with the prospect of playing with the toy.

2 ▷▷
Throw the toy
Once your dog is excited, throw the toy for him to chase and capture. It is best to do this in a familiar area, where it is quiet and there are no distractions.

3 △

"Well done!"

As soon as your dog picks up the toy, praise him, continuing to do so for as long as he carries it. Do not touch the toy. If your dog comes to you, praise him and stroke his back and body, avoiding the head and neck.

4 ▷

Dropped it

If your dog drops the toy, stop all praise. Either encourage him to pick the toy up by pointing at it and making encouraging noises, or pick it up and repeat steps 1 and 2.

GOOD PRACTICE

Some dogs enjoy possessing a toy while others like to chase it. Working out what your dog prefers will help you to make this game more enjoyable.

Keep the toys you practise the retrieve with special by hiding them from your dog at times when you are not playing.

Control reduces enthusiasm, so at this stage avoid any control, such as asking your dog to sit first, and just try to create as much excitement and enthusiasm for the exercise as possible.

Your attitude during this exercise is important. You need to be encouraging and enjoying yourself. Only try this when you are in a good mood and full of energy!

Outdoor enthusiasm
Try to excite your dog to the same level of enthusiasm whether you are in your garden, in the park, or out for a walk.

Retrieve 2

When your dog plays enthusiastically with a toy and carries it readily, it is time to ask her to bring it back to you. This exercise builds on the steps learned in Retrieve 1 (pp.136–7) and introduces the "drop" command.

Teaching your dog to retrieve forms the basis for more advanced training exercises, such as chase recall (pp.154–5). While some dogs retrieve easily, any dog can be taught this skill with sufficient practice. It is important to be patient throughout your training sessions as you can easily teach your dog to avoid you if you try to pry the toy from her mouth before she is ready to release it.

"Good dog!"

1 △
Encourage retrieval
Throw a toy and encourage your dog to pick it up. Then move backwards enthusiastically, coaxing her to come towards you.

2 ◁
Praise well
Keep still and let your dog approach you. Stroke her body, keeping your hands away from her head and neck. Continue to praise her until she begins to lose interest in holding the toy.

3 ▽
Reel her in
If your dog refuses to come near you while holding the toy, use a long training lead to bring her to you, coaxing her forward as you do so.

"**Never chase a dog** when you want **to get a toy back.**"

"Drop!"

4 ◁
Letting go
Once your dog comes to you readily with the toy in her mouth, you can teach her to drop it on command. Tease her with another toy, or offer her a treat. At the same time, say "drop", pointing at the ground, and wait until she decides to let go.

5 △
Trade and treat
As soon as she drops the toy, praise her warmly, then throw the other toy for her to fetch or feed the treat, continuing your praise.

GOOD PRACTICE

If your dog comes to you with a toy in her mouth, don't grab it from her. Dogs are very sensitive to our body language and she will instinctively try to protect her toy, especially if she has had it taken away from her on a previous occasion. You need to build her trust to get her to bring the toy to you and give it up willingly.

Never chase a dog when you want her to give up a toy. Most dogs are faster and more agile than their owners, and you are unlikely to catch up.

If your dog is attached to a long line while you are teaching this exercise, be gentle as you bring her towards you and take care not to get tangled in it. Make sure there are no children, vulnerable people, or other dogs close by.

Don't grab
Teaching the retrieve requires patience, so resist the urge to grab the toy out of your dog's mouth, as it will only delay her learning.

Developing the retrieve

Once your dog will retrieve well, you can refine his skills by teaching him to wait while a toy is thrown, to deliver the toy to your hand rather than dropping it on the ground, and to pick up objects other than toys.

Teaching your dog to wait while a toy is thrown will give you more control in times of excitement. A dog that learns to give toys directly to your hand is much easier to play with. Learning to pick up stationary objects and objects other than toys lays the foundation for further interesting exercises, such as carry the shopping (pp.176–7), fetch the lead (178–9), and put the toys away (180–1).

2 ▽ ▷
Retrieve
Once the toy has landed, ask your dog to fetch and, at the same time, drop one end of the line so he is free to go after the toy.

1 △
Wait
Loop a length of line through your dog's collar and hold both ends. Give a clear hand signal and ask your dog to wait (pp.128–9). Throw the toy a short distance. Use the line to hold your dog back if he tries to move forward.

"Always praise when your dog **brings** something **to you."**

◁ *"Fetch!"*
Teach your dog to fetch a non-moving object. Play a retrieval game with it first, then place the item on the floor and ask him to fetch.

△ **Appetizing exchange**
To teach your dog to deliver the toy to your hand, ask him to come right up to you, and praise him as he does so. When he is within reach, offer a tasty treat, and place your other hand underneath to catch the ball.

◁ **Tease**
To teach your dog to pick up something other than a toy, start by tying a soft item to it so that it feels similar. Tease him and play a fun game.

GOOD PRACTICE

When you first ask your dog to wait before fetching, make sure he is well exercised and throw an unexciting toy a short distance. Work up to asking him to wait to retrieve when he is full of energy and very excited about the prospect of giving chase.

Search and retrieve
You can train your dog to retrieve any number of things and in a variety of situations, including finding a lost set of keys in a field.

If your dog drops the ball before you have had a chance to take it, ask him to "fetch" again. Praise him while he holds the ball to let him know this is what you wanted. Then try the appetizing exchange (above) again, substituting the ball for a tasty treat. Your dog will soon learn that he will only earn the treat if he delivers the ball directly into your hand.

Advanced training

Developing skills

Showing off

Housework

Best behaviour

Developing skills

Well-trained dogs make walks and daily exercise sessions a pleasure. Teaching your dog to **come back when called, whatever he is doing** or whatever is going on around him, takes time, but it is really **worth the effort.** Training him to **check in with you** before running to meet strangers or other dogs gives you **more control,** and stops him being a nuisance to other walkers. Educating your dog to **stop chasing,** especially if he has strong chase instincts, and to **sit at a distance,** keeps him in check and could even save his life. This section **builds on your basic training,** and helps you to **teach your dog** some **really useful life skills.**

REALITY TRAINING
Training basic exercises in real-life scenarios will result in a dog that knows how to behave well in all situations and circumstances.

Advanced recalls 1

Once you have taught the basic recall (pp.124–5), it is important to teach your dog to come back to you even when she is busy doing other things, so that she learns to respond to you no matter what the situation.

Training your dog to return to you whatever the circumstances is a valuable and potentially life-saving command for your dog to learn. Dogs like to explore and greet other dogs during a walk, and it is important that you can get them back quickly if necessary. Remember to reward generously during your training sessions to make the experience as positive as possible for your dog.

"Come!"

1 △
Play a game
Ask a friend to play an exciting game with your dog and her favourite toy a few metres from where you are standing.

2 ◁
Interrupt play
Call your dog loudly to interrupt the play. As soon as your friend hears you call, she needs to stop playing with the toy and hide it from the dog's sight.

3 ▽
Recall and reward
Keep calling until your dog comes to you – it is important that both of you ignore her until she does. When she reaches you, praise her well and feed her a tasty treat.

"Practise this exercise **at home, and then on walks,** until your dog regularly **comes to you as soon** as you call."

4 ▷

Release

When your dog has successfully responded to your call, allow her to return to her game, so that she learns that coming to you is just a pleasant interruption, rather than an end to her enjoyment.

5 ◁

Rehearse

After a few practice sessions, your dog will learn that her game is over until she has come to you when you've called. She will begin to leave her play as soon as you start to call.

GOOD PRACTICE

In your first few training sessions, call when your friend is holding the toy but your dog is not touching it. Slowly work up to calling when your dog is holding onto the toy as her recall reliability improves.

Remember to keep training sessions short so your dog does not lose focus.

Make sure you have irresistible treats for this exercise, as your dog deserves to be rewarded generously and consistently for leaving an enjoyable game.

If you are struggling to make this exercise work, lower the excitement level of the game and find more enticing treats (p.108). Some dogs may prefer a more exciting game as a reward for coming when called.

Hot dog!
Because this exercise involves energy-sapping games, practise in short sessions so your dog does not get exhausted, particularly on hot days.

Advanced recalls 2

Once your dog comes back easily when you call him away from a game with a toy, the next step is to teach him to come back from other exciting activities, such as sniffing interesting smells and playing with other dogs.

Doing this gives you a reliable recall, no matter what your dog happens to be doing at the time. It will also make walks safer and allow him more freedom. Begin with distractions that are easy to break away from, such as sniffing, and only call if there is a good chance that your dog will come back to you. In this way, you can slowly build up the level of distraction until he comes back to you regardless.

△ **Distract him**
Wait until your dog is really interested in a scent, then call him excitedly, moving away from him and putting lots of effort into getting him to return. Reward him generously when he does.

▷ **Safety first**
If your dog is not yet trained or he is in a place where he could get into trouble, use a long line to allow him to exercise safely. Take care not to get tangled up in the line.

GOOD PRACTICE

You need your best treats for these exercises as you will have to compete for your dog's attention with very exciting events.

Some dogs prefer games with toys to treats. Use whatever rewards work during training sessions, and don't

Use a long line
If your dog will not leave other dogs when you call, use a long line to bring him to you, reward him well, and then let him go and play again.

forget to praise your dog well when he comes back to you.

When you start practising recalls from distraction, call your dog when you are close to him, as it is more likely that he will respond. As he gets better at recalls, call him from further away and increase the number and types of distractions competing for his attention.

1 ◁

Playtime

Play with another dog is very exciting, so it is unlikely that you will be able to call your dog away from these games during the first fun-filled minutes. Allow them to play and wait until the excitement levels are lower.

2 ▽

Successful call

Call at a moment when play has subsided and your dog can be distracted. Call loudly and enthusiastically, moving back and rattling food bags or squeaking a toy to attract him.

3 ▷

Reward well

Reward your dog really well for coming to you. Use your highest-value food treats and games, together with plenty of praise, to ensure success next time you call. Then let him return to his games with the other dog.

Checking in

Teaching your dog to check in with you before running to greet strangers or other dogs while out on walks allows you to control such situations and avoid any problems that may otherwise arise.

Before you begin teaching your dog to check in with you, she must have learned the basic recall exercise (pp.124–5). Training your dog to return to you before running to meet new people or other animals will help to keep her safe from any potentially dangerous dogs and will also prevent her from causing undue stress when encountering people who may be wary of dogs.

"Call your dog if you see **unfamiliar dogs or people approaching."**

1 △

Really sociable
A well-socialized dog will want to run and greet other dogs and their owners she sees while you are exercising her.

2 ▷

Recall
Before your dog gets too close to the approaching dog and owner, call her back to you. If your dog does not return immediately, work on her recall reliability by calling her to you as soon as you see someone approaching in the distance.

3 ▷
"Good girl!"
Reward your dog with effusive praise and her favourite treats or a game for returning to you. Always reward your dog well for responding to your call.

4 ◁
Careful greeting
If you think it is appropriate, you can now allow your dog to greet the other dog and her owner. It is usually best if the dogs are allowed to meet off lead and are able to sniff each other.

GOOD PRACTICE

This technique is particularly useful if your dog is large or looks intimidating, especially if she is naturally friendly with either people or other dogs.

Practise this exercise until your dog automatically checks in with you when she sees someone approaching.

It is better if dogs meet off lead if possible. However, if the other dog is on a lead, attach a lead to your dog, and keep your dog away to prevent her from scaring the other dog, who is restricted. Similarly, if your dog is likely to jump up, put her on a lead so that you can control her movements and prevent her from alarming or jumping up on the other person.

Ignoring others
If you don't think a meeting is appropriate, keep your dog on the lead and keep her gaze focused on you until the distraction has passed.

Sit at a **distance**

Sit at a distance is easy to train once you have taught your dog to sit on cue, and it is a useful way to get him to stop when he is away from you. This helps to keep him safe, and could save his life in an emergency.

This exercise can be taught once your dog will sit readily on cue (pp.122–3), either in front or beside you, in any situation, and with distractions going on around you (pp.114–5). Your dog may experience confusion at first, because previous rewards came for sitting near to you. You need to be patient to give him time to understand what you are asking him to do.

1 ◁
Ask him to sit
With a friend holding your dog's lead, stand just in front and ask him to sit. Give the hand signal to help him get it right, and reward him when he sits.

2 ▽
Move back
Take two paces back from your dog and repeat stage 1, again using the hand signal and rewarding him when he sits.

GOOD PRACTICE

The sit at a distance exercise can be used in emergencies when you want your dog to stop immediately – for example, if a child nearby has become frightened of him running around, or if a car unexpectedly approaches. Always go to reward him where he is sitting, so he learns to keep still.

Remember to begin training this exercise in a quiet location with no distractions. As your dog learns the concept of sitting at a distance, begin training in areas that offer more distractions, where he will find it more difficult to concentrate.

You can teach your dog to lie down at a distance in the same way. This is a more reliable position for some dogs.

Safety stop
Being able to stop your dog successfully when he is approaching danger is important. It is also useful when it is not safe to recall him.

"The **sit at a distance** exercise can be used in **emergencies."**

5. ▽
Practise
Progress slowly, gradually moving further away from your dog over several sessions. Eventually, you can dispense with your friend's assistance, but start again from stage 1 when you do so.

3. △
Lure but don't reward
If your dog does not respond, ask your friend to lure him into a sit (pp.122–3), but not to feed the treat to your dog at this point.

4. ▷
Now reward
Move forward quickly to reward him. He will soon learn the reward comes from you when he sits.

Chase recall

Being able to recall your dog from a chase is essential if you want him to be under complete control and safe to let off the lead. Begin by teaching him a chase recall using toys, and progress to other things he may chase.

This exercise is an important lesson for all dogs, and especially for breeds in which the chase instinct is accentuated. Teaching the chase recall with toys gives you the foundation of this exercise.

You can then progress to practising in real life situations, near things your dog is likely to chase, such as bicycles or other animals, to ensure that you have complete control when you really need it.

Advanced training

1 △
Line up
Ask a friend to help you. Position her so that she is facing you at a distance from where she can easily catch a ball that you throw.

2 ▷
Throw the ball
Tease your dog with the toy, then throw it past your friend for your dog to chase. Throw the toy at a height and speed that allows your friend to catch it if necessary.

3. ▽

Catch

For one in five throws at random, throw the toy so that your friend catches it and tucks it out of sight. As the toy leaves your hand, shout "leave!".

"As the **toy** leaves your **hand,** shout 'leave!'."

4. △

Throw another ball

When your dog looks back at you to get help in finding the ball, tease him with a toy he prefers and throw it in the opposite direction for him to chase.

GOOD PRACTICE

Only stop your dog running out after the toy once in every five throws at random. If you stop him more than this, he will become hesitant about running out after the ball and you will lose his enthusiasm.

Don't run your dog to the point of exhaustion. Up to 20 chases are enough for one session depending on the fitness level of the dog and how warm the weather is. Because you can only stop him four times in 20 chases, the opportunities to learn the chase recall are limited, so be patient and keep practising until he learns what to do.

Once your dog has learned to stop chasing a toy as soon as you call, set up other chase scenarios so you can practise recalling him, for example with joggers or bicycles. Use a training line for safety until you are sure of success.

"Stop!"
Achieve the same goal by stopping your dog as he runs past you towards the toy. Step forward and stop him verbally. As he stops, throw another toy.

Learning with distractions

Once your dog has learned basic lessons at home, teach him to respond to your cues in a variety of places, with different things happening around him. Begin with small distractions and progress to larger ones.

Training your dog in the safety of your home is a good place to begin. However, if this is the only place you teach in, this is the only place where your dog will behave well. You need to train your dog in a range of situations, so he learns to be responsive everywhere, regardless of distractions. Also teach him to respond when he would rather be doing something else, and reward him well for doing so.

◁ *Stay close*
Getting, and keeping, your dog's attention while other dogs play nearby takes practice. Start far enough away for him to concentrate, using rewards to lessen the appeal of the other dogs, and gradually move closer to them.

▽ *Back to basics*
Even if your dog usually walks beside you on the lead without pulling, don't expect him to do so when another dog is present. Teach him as before (pp.132–5) until he remembers what to do.

◁ *Wait for greeting*
Instil good manners with visitors by keeping your dog on a lead and teaching him to sit and wait until you are ready for him to greet them. Practise with friends until he is reliable.

"Many owners only **train** their dogs in **one location,** which can mean the **dogs do not respond** in **real-life situations."**

▷ *Car safety*
Teach your dog to sit and wait when the car door is opened, until you are ready for him to jump out. Practise this until he waits automatically. This could help prevent an accident.

▽ *Tricks anywhere*
If you ask your dog to perform a trick in a different place with other people watching, he may forget what to do. Patiently return to the basics, so he knows what to do next time.

GOOD PRACTICE

When you begin practising in a different place with distractions, remember to start the exercise again from scratch as if you were teaching it for the first time. Be patient and consistent, and gently insist that your dog does as you ask. If necessary, temporarily move further away from the distractions until he is able to concentrate.

If your dog finds working in some environments stressful, you may need to habituate him to that situation until he is at ease there before starting training.

Start again
Your dog may readily respond to the cues you give, but other members of the family may need to teach him from the beginning.

Dogs enjoy their owner's laughter and excitement, and both you and your dog will have **lots of fun learning** the **tricks** in this section. These exercises help to use up your dog's **mental energy** and **give him a purpose**, resulting in a more **relaxed, contented animal.** They are **impressive** when shown to friends, and can be added to a training session to give **variety** and to **lighten the mood.** Once dogs have learned the tricks well, they really seem to **enjoy the performance,** especially when in front of an appreciative audience. This section will further **improve your training skills,** and give you a more **versatile dog** that knows many useful cues.

FINE PERFORMANCE
Once dogs are accomplished at a trick, they will enjoy performing it, especially if their efforts are rewarded well at the end.

Wave

It is easy to teach your dog to wave, and this exercise is a good place to start your trick training. A wave can make a big dog look friendly and less intimidating to children and it is also a great way to say goodbye to guests.

Teaching the wave exercise requires patience. Your dog will need time to think things through, so don't be tempted to rush through the stages. Keep sessions short and successful and, if necessary, go back a step in order to end with something easy. If your dog jumps up to get the treat, or does something similarly undesirable, patiently reposition him and try again.

1 ▷
Incentive to paw
Wrapping a treat in your hand, let your dog smell the treat, and encourage him to paw at your hand by moving it around at floor level. Reward any slight movements of his paw immediately, and wait patiently for him to touch your hand with his paw.

"Keep sessions short… if required, go back a step."

2 ◁
Rewarding touch
Once your dog knows he has to touch your hand with his paw for you to release the treat, begin to move your hand slowly off the ground over several sessions.

3 ▷
Higher still
When you raise the treat higher than your dog can reach, you will need to be patient to get him to raise his paw. Reward any slight movement of his paw at first and ask for more in later sessions.

4 ▷
And wave
Practise, raising your hand even higher and rewarding "waves" immediately. In later sessions, introduce a hand signal and voice cue. Train in different places, with distractions and with your dog in varying positions in relation to you.

Spin

An easy trick to teach, the spin is a very useful warm-up exercise before competing in active dog sports (pp.232–3). Most dogs really enjoy performing the spin and will do it readily when asked by their owners.

Make sure you teach your dog to spin in both directions to prevent her from becoming dizzy and also to avoid muscle building up on one side only. Take care with young, active dogs who may spin obsessively once they find out how much fun this activity is.

1 △
Follow the lure
Holding a treat just in front of your dog's nose, lure her around and away from you in a circle. Move slowly so she can follow you easily.

2 ▷
Reward halfway
Reward your dog as she passes the halfway point of the circle, so she understands it is worth her while to follow the lure again next time.

3 △
Reward the full circle
Keep luring your dog round until she has moved full circle and is back in the starting position, facing you. Reward her well.

4 ▷
Spin!
Practise this routine together over several training sessions, gradually phasing out the halfway reward until you only reward a full spin. Eventually, you will be able to build your lure into a hand signal (pp.110–11).

GOOD PRACTICE

Over several sessions, try to build in more spins before rewarding your dog.
If you want to put the action on voice cue (pp.110–11), choose a different word for each direction – for example, "spin" and "twirl" – to avoid confusion.

Clockwise
Once your dog fully understands how to spin in one direction and does so readily, you can start to train him to spin in the other direction as well.

Anticlockwise
When training your dog to spin the other way, start from stage one again, luring him in the other direction until he understands what to do.

Hi-five

The hi-five is a favourite trick for many dogs and their owners. It is advisable to teach this in preference to shaking a paw, as some dogs can find it quite threatening to have their paw lifted and held.

It is a good idea to teach your dog to wave (pp.160–1) before attempting the hi-five, as the early stages of training are similar. Once she can wave with ease, you can build on her skills with this exercise.

2 ▽

Open one hand
Hold out your other hand just above the floor, so that when your dog lifts her paw, it lands on your open hand instead of the hand holding the treat. Reward her well.

3 △

Raise your hand
Practise this motion, raising your hand a little higher each time. Move the hand with the treat to encourage her, and reward her well as soon as she makes contact with her paw.

1 △

Hold a treat to the floor
Wrap a treat in your hand and move it about in front of her, encouraging her to paw at your hand as she tries to get the treat. Reward her as soon as she makes contact and practise over several sessions.

GOOD PRACTICE

When your dog successfully performs a hi-five and touches your hand with her paw, take care that you support the paw lightly rather than trying to hold on to it, as this may cause her to withdraw it.

Practise the hi-five in a range of different places and with a variety of distractions going on around you. If your dog forgets what you are asking her to do in an unfamiliar location or in front of an audience, gently remind her by going through the stages above.

Teach your dog to respond to a voice command to help her distinguish the hi-five from the wave. Say "hi-five", wait a moment, then hold up your hand as before. Always reward her well for putting her paw against your hand.

Crouching hi-five
At first, you will need to kneel down or crouch. As your dog becomes more proficient, you will be able to teach him to "hi-five" while you stand.

4 △

Hi-five!
Repeat the exercise over several sessions, building in the hi-five signal with your hand upright and palm facing your dog, until she learns to place her paw against your raised hand to get her reward.

5 ◁

Timely offering
Once your dog readily places her paw against your hand, introduce a pause between contact and reward. Start to extend this gap so that her paw is pressed against your palm for longer periods.

Play dead

Play dead is a fun trick to show friends and, when combined with a hand signal in the shape of a gun and a spoken "bang!", can look impressive, especially if your dog will lie motionless with her head down and tail still.

Once your dog has learned the down position (pp.126–7), it is usually quite easy to teach her to lie flat on her side and completely still. However, it takes more time and repetition for her to learn how to fall flat from a standing position. She may fall fast or "die" slowly. Reviving her with "medicine", in the form of a tasty treat, rewards the behaviour and gives the exercise a positive conclusion.

> **"Don't laugh** or react if your **dog lifts her head** up. Wait until she is 'dead' again before **rewarding."**

1 △
Relax
Ask your dog to lie down. Using a large tasty treat, lure her head slowly round to the side. Be patient and let your dog lick and chew at the treat until she relaxes and rolls her hips to one side.

2 ▷
Head swivel
Slowly move the treat around, so that your dog's head turns and her nose moves towards her tail. Allow her to chew the treat and let her relax until her weight is resting on one hip and one front leg.

3

Praise gently

Slowly move the treat in an arc in front of your dog until her head is on the floor and she is lying flat. Feed the treat and praise her gently. Ask her to "stay" and feed another treat. Practise over several sessions until you can lure her into position and she lies flat while you get up.

4

Play dead

With your dog in the down position, say "bang!" and give your hand signal while standing. Then lure her into position and reward her well. After several sessions, give the cue and wait for a response – help her with the lure only if necessary.

GOOD PRACTICE

Don't laugh or react if your dog lifts her head off the floor. Wait until she is "dead" again before rewarding.

Progress to teaching your dog to play dead from a standing position. Give your voice cue and hand signal as above, then wait for the count of two for a response. If none is forthcoming, use a treat to lure her into down (don't say anything else at this stage), then into a "lie flat" position. Reward her, then stand up, then reward her again so she knows that you want her to lie flat and stay still.

Repeat these stages until your dog learns what is required of her. As soon as she plays dead for the first time, reward her with a treat and praise her well, then end the session, practising again later.

Falling down
Once your dog has learned to respond to the cue while lying down, teach her to play dead from a stand. This should be easy with regular practise.

Jump

Teaching your dog to jump is a really useful training exercise, making life easier for you as you will not have to lift her over any obstacles. Start slowly and build up gradually to develop your dog's confidence.

It is important to protect a young puppy's growing joints and limbs, so only teach this exercise to dogs over 12 months old who are fully developed. Make sure that your dog is physically fit and has no joint or health problems before asking her to jump. Hip and elbow dysplasia are common in pedigree dogs and often go undetected until later in life. If your dog is reluctant to jump, ask your vet for advice.

1 △
Excite her
For this exercise, you need a jump pole and adjustable stands. Begin by placing the jump pole on the ground. With your dog on a lightweight lead, tease her with a ball or a toy until she is excited and wants to chase after it.

2 ▽
Throw the ball
Toss the ball in a low arc over the pole. Ask your dog to "jump", pointing to the pole so she learns to follow your hand signal, and stepping forwards to encourage her. Release the lead as she moves to fetch the toy.

3 △
Raise the jump and try again
Raise the pole by 5cm (2in) and repeat the first two stages. Over several sessions, gradually raise the pole higher. Don't forget to release the lead as your dog races after the toy and jumps.

4 △

No running out

If your dog tries to go round or under the jump, use the lead to prevent her. Go back to where you started and try again. Ask for no more than three jumps per session and remember to get her excited before you throw the toy.

5 ▷

Jump!

Once your dog learns what is required, encourage her to jump first, then throw the ball later as a reward. When she no longer tries to go around the jump, dispense with the lead.

GOOD PRACTICE

As you ask your dog to jump a little bit higher, make sure that she starts far enough back to clear the jump.

If your dog falls when jumping, lower the jump considerably before trying again. Reward a successful jump at the lower height before you gradually raise the pole again to make it harder.

Jumping is very tiring for your dog, and uses unusual muscles, so keep sessions short. Encourage her to do a few jumps and then wait until the next training session before you ask her to do more.

Jumping is a necessary skill for many dog sports, particularly agility (pp.234–7). To build a good foundation for later speed and accuracy, take things slowly and ensure success at each height.

Useful trick
Once your dog has learned how to jump, he will be able to negotiate real life obstacles, such as gates and fences.

Take a message

As its name implies, this exercise involves training your dog to pass a message between you and another person. It is simple to teach once your dog has learned to retrieve and give things up (pp.136–9), and is great fun.

Teach this exercise indoors over several sessions, and ask a person your dog is familiar with to assist. Start by using a short distance between you and the person who will receive the message. Then build up longer distances, with the other person in different rooms in the house. Help your dog if necessary in the early stages, walking towards the message's recipient if your dog seems confused.

"If your **dog drops** the **message, encourage** him to **pick it up** again. **Never** get cross or **tell him off for dropping the paper.**"

3 ▷

En route
Encourage him in the direction of a friend nearby, pointing to her and saying "take it!" enthusiastically. Ask your friend to call your dog and urge him to move towards her.

1 △

Fetch games
Begin by getting your dog used to the feel of paper in his mouth by playing fetch games (pp.136–9). Expect to get through lots of paper, but practise until he will retrieve the "message" from the floor and bring it back to you readily.

2 ▷

Give him the message
Once your dog has learned to take hold of the message and carry it in his mouth, get his attention and hand him the message to hold.

4 △
"Well done!"
Ask the recipient to exchange the message for a treat as soon as your dog reaches her, keeping the treat out of sight until he is very close. She should then feed the treat and praise him well, so that he knows he has done the right thing.

5 △
Make it harder
Practise over several sessions until your dog knows what to do. Then gradually increase the distance between you and the message recipient, asking her to hide around the corner and, eventually, in other parts of the house.

GOOD PRACTICE

If your dog drops the "message", encourage him to pick it up again, sliding the paper across the floor if necessary to make it more exciting for him to pick up. Once he does so, praise him continuously while he grasps the paper in his mouth, making sure that he knows how clever he is. Never get cross or tell him off for dropping the paper.

A more advanced version of this game is to teach your dog the names of other family members or friends. You can then ask him to take the message to a named individual. First, teach your dog the names of different people by practising repeatedly until he knows which person to give the message to when everyone is sitting in the same room. Once he has learned everyone's names, locating and giving a message to an individual elsewhere in the house will be easy.

Find the lost toy

Hide and seek games are very easy for your dog to play, because they require a good sense of smell. Once she knows how to play them, these games are fun and will help to use up her energy.

This is a good game to play inside. Once you have taught your dog to find an item hidden somewhere in your home, you can relax while your dog hunts for it. However, you must be on hand to help her if she can't find the toy, and don't tease her by asking her to search for something that isn't there.

1 ▷
"Fetch!"
Start by playing fun retrieval games (pp.136–41) with a new toy in short sessions over several days, until it becomes your dog's favourite toy and she runs to fetch it wherever you decide to throw it.

> **"Reduce** the **help you give** until she can **find** a **toy hidden** anywhere."

2 △
Hide the toy
Ask your dog to sit and wait, then wave the toy in front of her to get her attention, before hiding it somewhere nearby where she can find it quite easily.

GOOD PRACTICE

At first, you will have to help your dog to find a toy that is hidden in another room. Go into the room and give the "find it!" cue, pointing towards the hiding place to encourage your dog to search the area that you are indicating. Slowly reduce the help you offer her over several sessions, until she can find a toy hidden anywhere in the room.

Over time, you can progress to hiding a variety of toys in different areas around your home. Make the search more challenging gradually, so that your dog knows exactly what to do and becomes an enthusiastic hunter.

Hand signal
Point your dog in the right direction by using a direct signal. Once he hunts for the toy on the cue "find it!", you no longer need to point.

3.

"Find it!"

Ask your dog to "find it!," pointing her towards the hiding place to direct her. Encourage her to keep searching until she has found the hidden toy, and then be sure to praise her well as soon as she has located it.

4.

Praise her

Ask your dog to bring the toy to you and let her know how clever she is as she does so. When she gives you the toy, reward her with a treat and lots of praise before hiding it again, this time in a different place, for her to find.

5.

Make it harder

You can gradually build up many different hiding places for the toy in rooms around your home, pointing her in the right direction to help her.

Housework

Dogs thrive on a sense of belonging and shared activity. As much of our lives are based in and around our homes, **training our dogs to help us with daily chores** is a good way to **make them feel included.** This also creates **more free time,** which you can spend with them. This section shows you how to teach your dog some **simple exercises** that will **allow him to help you with the housework** – for example, tidying up his own toys. As you teach the exercises, **you will learn valuable training skills.** You can then build on these skills to teach your dog to be involved in other projects and tasks around the home that will be **useful** to you, and **fun** for him.

WILLING WORKER
Dogs really enjoy it when they are rewarded well for working. It will ensure that they are ready and willing to help you with the chores.

Carry the shopping

It is really useful to have some assistance when you have too much to carry, and your dog is sure to enjoy helping you with this simple household task. It will strengthen your relationship and make him feel valued.

Once your dog knows how to fetch and pick up toys when asked (pp.136–41), teaching him to carry in the shopping is relatively easy. When he has learned this, you can extend it to other jobs in the home, such as carrying in the washing. Start off by making it easy for him to learn to pick up awkward but manageable objects by playing retrieve games with a variety of empty packets and containers.

1.▽

Play a game
Tease your dog with an ordinary household object, such as an empty plastic bottle, to get him interested in playing a game. Keep moving it around until he wants to grab hold of it.

3.▽

Make it harder
Once he can carry empty bottles and packets, progress to asking him to carry full ones. Over several sessions, he will learn what is required and you will be able to hand him objects to hold rather than throwing them for him to pick up.

2.△

Praise him
Roll the bottle along the floor to encourage your dog to chase and pick it up. Once he has, praise him enthusiastically. Over several sessions, slowly build up to asking him to walk with you while he holds the bottle.

"When he has learned to **carry shopping,** teach him to **help you with other household chores,** such as **carrying in the washing.**"

4 ◁

Carry the shopping
Progress to asking him to carry an easy item, such as a lightweight bag, over a short distance. If he drops it, ask him to "fetch" and reduce the distance. Praise frequently.

5 △

"Thank you!"
Ask him to wait while you put down your bags. Take the item he is carrying from him, then praise him really well and quickly find a tasty treat to reward him.

GOOD PRACTICE

If your dog chews the object you give him, let him play with another empty packet of a similar texture. Dogs use chewing as a way of exploring an object, just as we use our hands to touch things. Giving your dog more opportunities to chew an item will eventually stop him doing so as he becomes familiar with it.

Once your dog fetches and carries items easily, ask him to help you around the house, finding and bringing different things to you. Don't give him breakable things to carry, or anything too heavy or sharp. Make it easy for him to understand what you want, and praise and reward him well. Most dogs love working in this way, and it will help to use up your dog's energy and keep him entertained.

Useful hound
You can make your dog feel really useful – and put your feet up in the evening – by training him to fetch your newspaper or your slippers.

Fetch the lead

Teaching your dog to fetch his lead is easy once he has learned to pick up toys and other items (pp.136–41). It will give him something fun to do while you get ready to go out for a walk.

Rewarding your dog with a walk every time he responds to your request to fetch his lead will soon have him racing to get it. After a while, he may even learn to anticipate your request, fetching it without being asked to do so whenever he sees you putting on your coat or preparing to go out. You can begin teaching him this assignment by playing some exciting retrieve games with the lead.

1. ▽
Folded and fastened
Make it easy for your dog to pick up the lead and carry it in his mouth by tying it in a knot. Over several sessions, practise throwing it and ask him to "fetch" until he readily retrieves it.

3. ▽
Encourage him
When your dog can carry the lead succesfully, place it on the ground near its usual hanging or storage place and ask him to "fetch". Reward him well when he brings it to you. Repeat the exercise over several sessions in this location.

2. △
Full length
Once your dog can carry a folded and tied lead, play some games with it untied. Initially, he may find it more difficult to carry and may tread on the trailing end, but he will improve with practice.

"Fetch!"

4. ▽
Lead position
Loop the lead, with the clip end close to the ground, over the peg or handle on which it usually hangs. This will prevent the clip landing on your dog's nose when he pulls it down. Ask him to "fetch".

5. ▷
Praise him
When your dog brings the lead to you, make sure that you tell him what a good boy he is and praise him well. Reward him with one of his favourite treats and then take him out for a walk to celebrate his success.

> **"Reward your dog** with a **walk** every time he **fetches his lead** – he will soon **race to get it."**

GOOD PRACTICE

Make sure that you hang your dog's lead on something secure, so that it won't fall on him when he pulls at it or moves in any way. This might frighten him and prevent him pulling at the lead again.

If your dog fetches the lead when you haven't asked for it, in anticipation of a walk, you should take it without praising or rewarding him and then return it to where he found it. Repeat until he gives up bringing it to you. Laughing, scolding, or giving in and taking him for a walk when he does this will only result in him doing it more often and, eventually, this will become a nuisance. However, he is trying to tell you something, so take note that he wanted to go for a walk when you didn't ask him, and make an effort to play more with him or take him out for walks more often.

You should always try to keep your dog's lead in the same place, so that he knows exactly where it is, and can fetch it easily when you ask him to.

Muted
Fetching and holding the lead is a good skill to teach if your dog is likely to bark with excitement at the thought of a walk. It's not possible to bark and hold the lead!

Put the toys away

Many toys may get scattered over the floor in the course of playing games with your dog. It makes sense to train her to tidy up her own toys and put them away. She will enjoy doing this if you reward her well for her efforts.

Placing a toy inside a box is not as natural a behaviour for a dog as taking it out, so this trick requires patient teaching and plenty of practice. Teach your dog to retrieve first (pp.136–41) and practise until it is easy for her to fetch items that are lying on the floor. This trick looks impressive and is really useful, especially when visitors are expected and you have little time to tidy before they arrive.

1 ▷

"Come!"
Throw a toy for your dog to fetch and call her to you as soon as she picks it up. Position yourself so that the box is between you and your dog, thereby making her come towards the box to get to you.

2 ▽

Bring the toy
As she comes closer, hold out your hand over the box and ask your dog to deliver the toy into your hand. Reward her well. Repeat over several sessions until she learns to do this easily.

> **"The reward** on offer must **outweigh the pleasure** of **holding on to the toy."**

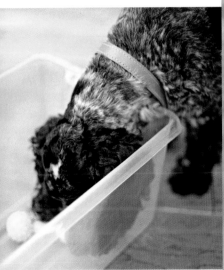

3 △

Find the treat

When she comes to you holding the toy and is over the box, drop a treat into the box. She will have to drop the toy into the box in order to find the treat. Practise this, giving her the cue "tidy up" as you send her for the toy.

4 ▷

Put the toys away

Ask your dog to "tidy up" but do not put any treats in the box. When she lifts her head after a fruitless search, reward her really well with treats and praise.

GOOD PRACTICE

If your dog drops the toy on the way to the box, withhold the treat and praise, and ask her to "fetch" again. Do not get cross or pressure her into doing it – just ask her nicely. It can take a long time for some dogs to learn to perform this trick successfully, so you must be patient and keep gently reminding your dog what you want her to do.

If your dog takes the toy out of the box again, make sure that the reward you are offering outweighs the pleasure of holding on to the toy (pp.206–7). Reward her with tastier treats or a favourite toy.

Repeat the steps above until your dog understands that she has to drop the toy into the box to be rewarded. Once she has learned this, you can gradually move further away from the box.

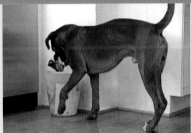

Rubbish collection

Once your dog has learned the principle of tidying up, ask him to put rubbish in the bin or washing in the laundry basket. Reward him well.

Go to bed

This is a useful exercise for occasions when you want your dog out of the way in a safe place, such as when you have visitors who do not like dogs, or when you are eating, dealing with a baby, or tackling tasks that require concentration.

This is easy to teach, but it can be tricky getting your dog to comply if she prefers to be with you. To teach her to respond in any circumstances, start slowly, asking her to go to bed when she would rather not. Make sure that she responds to your request, and that the reward outweighs the enjoyment she would get from doing what she prefers to do.

2 △
"Go to bed!"
Send your dog forwards to find the treat with the cue "go to bed". Try to send her from a direction that allows her to locate the treat while standing on her bed.

1 △
Place the treat
Ask your dog to sit, then wait (pp.128–9), or ask a friend to hold her. Show your dog that you have a tasty treat, and then place it behind her bed, so that it is within easy reach, but out of her sight.

"Spend time making this a **pleasant experience** for your dog with **treats** and **lots of praise."**

GOOD PRACTICE

Eventually, as your dog understands what you want when you ask her to "go to bed", you can dispense with the treat behind her bed altogether, and reward her only for lying down on the bed.

Steadily build up your dog's compliance by asking her to go to her bed and stay there, even when there are more interesting things going on around her.

3
Lie down
As soon as your dog has eaten the treat, move towards the bed. Say her name to get her attention, so that she turns around to face you, then ask her to lie down.

"Good girl!"

4 △
Enjoyable experience
Praise her well for lying down on her bed. Spend some time making this a pleasant experience with treats and fuss. Progress over several sessions, gradually increasing the distance between you and the bed.

If your dog refuses to go to bed, gently insist that she does as you ask, but make sure you ask in less distracting circumstances next time, so that you build up the skill more gradually.

Once your dog is reliably going to her bed when you ask her to, and staying there, you should reward her well for her good behaviour. Remember to go over to her periodically to reward her again for staying in place.

Soft option
Make sure that your dog's bed is comfortable and not too far from where you will be, so that she will be less tempted to come looking for you.

Distract her
To increase the chances that she will stay on her bed, give her something interesting to chew, so that she has a good reason to be there.

Shut the door

Teaching your dog to shut doors is both useful and impressive. It is more difficult to teach than most other tricks, so you need plenty of patience, but by breaking it down into small stages, you will be successful.

Start off by teaching your dog to touch a target by holding out a pen and rewarding him with a treat as soon as he touches the end with his nose. Continue practising this over several sessions until he will run to touch the end of the pen wherever it is held. You can then progress through further training sessions using a sticky note, attaching it first to the palm of your hand before progressing to a door.

3. ▽
Touch the paper!
Put the sticky note on a low door, point, and say "close the door". Wait patiently. If he does not touch it, stick it to your hand and hold it close to the door. Keep trying until he touches the door.

1. △
Target training
Hold a pen, call your dog, and reward him when he touches it with his nose. Once he does this reliably, add the voice cue "close the door" just before you present the pen.

2. ▷
Swap pen for paper
Attach a sticky note to your hand. Ask your dog to "close the door" and wait for him to touch it with his nose. Reward him instantly, and repeat over several sessions.

4 ◁

"Close the door!"
Once your dog has learned to push the door shut with the paper target attached, start to train him without. Begin your session with the paper, then, after two successful attempts, remove it and ask him to "close the door". Wait for him to shut the door, then reward him really well and end the session.

"Practise with **different doors** until he will **close any door** and run to you for a **reward."**

GOOD PRACTICE

If, during step 3, he does not push the door firmly, get him excited, then hold him back and ask him to "close the door", moving forward when you release him. His extra momentum will shut the door. Reward him with a jackpot (pp.116–7).

Pull the door shut
Play exciting tug games with a loop of material until your dog will readily pull it, then hang it on a door that opens outwards and ask him to "pull".

Never reward touches or pushes with a paw instead of the nose. This will result in scratched doors as your dog tries to close them with his paws instead.

When practising with different doors, always return to step 3 to make it easy for him to understand what you mean.

Best behaviour

A dog with good manners makes a popular pet and likeable companion that you will be happy to take out and about. Dogs that **jump up** at people, **snatch food** from their hands, **will not settle down, barge past people** to get through doorways first, **chase things** they should not, **bark excessively,** and **cannot be handled** easily are really **difficult to live with.** Learn how to **teach your dog good manners,** so that he does not do these things, and instead can live easily and **harmoniously** with you. Patiently teaching good manners at home, and then in all situations and circumstances, will result in a **well-behaved dog that is acceptable anywhere.**

CHASING DANGER
Inappropriate chases can get a dog and its owner into trouble. It is important to prevent this and use games as an outlet for excess energy.

No jumping

Dogs jump up to get closer to our faces in order to greet us, and to get our attention. It may be appealing when puppies do this, but it can become an irritating and dangerous habit in older dogs.

Everyone in the family, and those familiar with your dog, need to work together to teach him to greet people appropriately. By adopting the simple approach shown here every time your dog jumps up, he will learn that it is not a rewarding action, and will, eventually, cease to do it. If he is rewarded with attention for keeping all four feet on the floor when he meets you, he will learn to do this instead.

1 ◁
Bad habit
Don't encourage your dog to jump up to get attention – it can rapidly develop into a consistent and unpleasant habit.

2 △
Cold shoulder
If your dog jumps up, don't speak, look at him, or touch him. Turn away, folding your arms, and ignore him until he stops.

"Good boy!"

4.
▽

Greeting friends
Keep him on a lead if visitors arrive, to stop him from jumping up. They should only greet your dog when he is calm. If they are willing, ask them to follow the steps shown here.

3.
△

Reward
As soon as your dog has all four feet back on the ground, crouch down to his level and greet and praise him enthusiastically. If he tries to jump up again, stand up and repeat the exercise, turning away and calmly ignoring him until he does what you want.

"Crouching down to **his level** will enable your dog to get **closer** to you."

GOOD PRACTICE

Once you begin this process, it is very important that everyone familiar to your dog follows the same approach every time he jumps up. Don't touch him, speak, or look at him if he does jump. If you acknowledge this behaviour, you will be randomly rewarding him (pp.116–7), and the problem will get worse.

Be patient and consistent, as it may take several weeks before your actions have a positive effect and your dog stops jumping up. Progress may be slow initially – his behaviour will even get worse for a while – but suddenly, you will see an improvement (pp.118–9). Always reward your dog well when he keeps all four feet on the floor.

If you have already taught your dog to sit, asking him to do so before he has a chance to jump up may encourage improved behaviour, as you are giving him something to do that is incompatible with jumping. Get down to his level and reward his sit by praising him warmly.

Controlled enthusiasm
Puppies like to get close to our faces to greet us. Get down to your puppy's level, so that he can learn to greet you without having to jump up.

No snatching

Dogs snatch food if they think there is a chance they will lose it. Prevent this behaviour by teaching your dog to wait patiently for his reward.

This problem usually develops during puppyhood, when an inexperienced puppy accidentally bites at his owner's hand holding out some food. The owner may then begin to whisk the hand away, with the food still in it, to avoid being bitten. The inevitable consequences of this are that the puppy learns that he has to move fast in order to get the food being offered and learns to snatch.

▷ *Competition*
It is possible that another dog will snatch the treat, so dogs learn to be fast to make sure they get fed. This leads to accidents, however, where they grab their owner's hand as well as the treat.

△ *Keep your hand flat*
One solution is to offer the food on the flat of the hand. Tuck in the thumb and keep the hand flat to make it easier for him to take the food gently without biting. This is a good method to use if you have young children, as they find this technique easy.

GOOD PRACTICE

When teaching your dog not to snatch (opposite), only say "off" once and keep your hand really still until your dog moves away.

As you practise, stay calm and wait patiently until he takes his nose away from your hand. Do not say anything – let him learn the lesson for himself. Reward him well when he gives up and moves away from your hand.

If your dog uses his teeth in his early attempts to get the treat, wear an old leather glove to protect your hand.

If you have two dogs, train them to sit and wait separately, then ask them to sit apart, so you can feed them individually without either feeling the need to snatch.

Paws off!
If your dog paws at the hand that is holding the treat, raise it higher to stop him doing so, but not so high that he can't reach it with his mouth.

1 ▷

Off!

Teach your dog to calm down and wait for his food by hiding a tasty treat in your closed hand and holding it out for him. Say "off", keeping your hand still, and ignore his attempts to get to the treat.

2 ◁

Wait

Keep your hand still and wait until you feel a small gap open between your dog's nose and your hand as he draws back. Then open your hand and feed the treat immediately.

3 ▷

Reward patience

Practise this until your dog learns to back away from your hand to get you to release the treat. Eventually, he will wait patiently to be fed when you say "off".

Settle

Teaching your dog to settle down when you ask results in a dog with good manners that is acceptable anywhere. It is also useful when you are busy, such as when answering the telephone or talking to people in the street.

Before you begin training your dog to settle, he must first learn the down cue (pp.126–7). Start teaching him to settle at home, with your dog's bed positioned next to you. As your dog gets used to being asked to settle down beside you, and understands that he will be rewarded for resting calmly, you can progress to practising in less familiar surroundings – for example, at a friend's house.

1 △
Lie down
Attach a lead to your dog's collar and ask him to sit quietly beside you on his bed. Wait until he is relaxed, then ask him to lie down, luring him down with a treat if necessary.

2 ▷
Relax
Sit back in a chair and relax, praising him calmly and stroking him gently while he settles, so that he knows he has done the right thing. If he becomes restless and gets up, ask him to lie down again.

"Good boy!"

3.▽

Keep him occupied

Give your dog a chew (p.95) to help keep him busy while you sit near him, perhaps reading a book or watching television. Start by keeping him settled for a few minutes, gradually extending these sessions for longer periods.

4.△

Change location

Try this exercise at a friend's house, or somewhere else familiar. Once he is used to settling in a couple of familiar places, start to vary locations, building in distractions until he can settle anywhere when asked.

> "This is particularly useful **when you are busy** or need to concentrate on **other things.**"

GOOD PRACTICE

The settle exercise requires your dog to keep still, so make sure that he has had plenty of stimulating physical and mental activity before attempting this exercise, especially if he is young and lively.

"Settle" is different to "wait" (pp.128–9), in which your dog remains in one position.

This exercise allows him to change position, stretch out, and move around a little as long as he stays close to you and remains calm and quiet.

Slowly get him used to settling in different locations with varying distractions, until he can lie down and relax anywhere. This allows you to take him anywhere without fuss.

Out and about
Your dog will find it more difficult to settle when there are distractions nearby. Be patient and gently insist that he complies with your request.

No pushing

If your dog charges through a door ahead of you, he risks tripping you up or running into the path of traffic or other dangers outside that you are not aware of. Teaching him to sit and wait while you go out first is safer.

Dogs that learn to wait politely for their owners to go through doorways and entrances before them develop self-control and learn to have more respect for their owners. Apart from being good manners,

this will make life easier for you and will be appreciated by visitors. The method given here builds on the sit (pp.122–3) and wait (pp.128–9) exercises, which need to be taught first.

1 ▽

Temptation to barge
The anticipation of going out or somewhere new may cause your dog to push through doorways ahead of you. If he is allowed to do this, you will not be able to check first that it is safe for him to do so.

2 △

"Sit"
To teach your dog to wait, move in front of him to position yourself between him and the door, and then ask him to sit. Close the door if he tries to run out.

3 ▷

Wait, then proceed
Slowly open the door. If your dog moves, close the door quickly and ask him to sit again. Continue until you can take a step through the open door and your dog remains sitting.

4 ◁

Reward
Once you have passed through the doorway to the other side, turn round and praise your dog. Reward him really well for remaining in the sit position.

"Reward him for staying in the sit position."

5 ◁

Release
When you are ready, release your dog from his sitting position by asking him to come through the open doorway to join you. Practise this often until he waits at doors automatically.

"Come!"

GOOD PRACTICE

Always make sure that your dog is well exercised before you attempt to teach this skill. A tired dog is more likely to remain sitting than a lively, excited one.

If your dog repeatedly tries to rush through the door as you step forwards, you can use a lead to restrict his progress, then reposition him and try again. Be patient and persistent.

Under control
If you own more than one dog, it is important to keep them under control at all times. Teaching this exercise will help them to learn self-control when they are in a pack.

If you have more than one dog, only work with one at a time until each dog can do it perfectly whenever you ask. Then, try with two together, then three, patiently teaching them until they will all sit together for you to go through first.

Insisting that your dog calmly waits by the doorway and allows you to go through first will help him to realize that his needs do not always come before yours, and that you control the territory.

No chasing

Many dogs, especially hounds and herding breeds, enjoy chasing and can get into trouble by doing it inappropriately. They may collide with cars or cyclists, or whatever they are chasing may get scared and retaliate.

To prevent this happening, a dog's desire to chase needs to be channelled into acceptable alternative outlets. Teaching them to play games and to chase toys instead of people gives dogs the opportunity to continue enjoying the thrill of the chase in a safe way. In addition, unacceptable chases must be stopped, such as with cars, cyclists, joggers, and cats, and dogs must be taught a chase recall (pp.154–5).

◁ *Dangerous games*
The desire to chase is strong. As well as movement, fear of the noise and the smell of cars or machinery or the sudden shock of an approaching jogger or cyclist can cause dogs to want to chase them away.

▽ *In control*
If your dog chases, keep him on a lead and put some distance between you and whatever is being chased. If he is still excited, get further away until he relaxes.

▷ *Early lessons*
Puppies must learn not to chase children. Teach your puppy to play with toys instead, and keep him on a lead while children play around him. Ask your children to stand still if they are chased.

> **"Your** dog's desire to **chase** needs to be **channelled** into **games** with **toys."**

▷ **Resisting the urge**
If your dog chases things that either excite or worry him, such as cyclists, desensitize him by relaxing in a place where he can get used to them. Keep him on a lead while he watches them in the distance. Start off a long way away and gradually get closer.

◁ **Start young**
Start as you mean to go on. A puppy that does not learn to chase things inappropriately will not do it when he is an adult. Prevent him from behaving in this way, and teach him to play games with toys instead.

GOOD PRACTICE

Dogs develop their chasing preferences during puppyhood and adolescence, so we must make sure that they only chase toys, rather than inappropriate objects, during this stage in their lives. Try to play enough chase games with your dog each day to use up all his mental and physical energy. The amount of energy he has depends on his breed, age, and fitness. If he really enjoys chase games, teach him a chase recall (pp.154–5), so you can get him back if he is running into danger.

Some dogs are aggressive when they catch whatever they are chasing and may bite in excitement or frustration to prevent it moving. Use a lead or muzzle and seek professional help for your dog.

Born to chase
Sight hounds are bred to chase and their desire to do so is extremely strong. You must channel this desire into acceptable games with toys.

No barking

Dogs bark for many reasons, such as to guard property, or because they are excited, or want to attract your attention. Discovering why your dog barks and addressing the problem are key to changing his behaviour.

Most dogs need very little encouragement to bark and, in this way, they differ greatly from their wild ancestors, wolves, who very rarely bark. Some breeds, particularly the Terriers and guarding breeds, as well as some smaller breeds bred especially for the purpose of sounding the alarm, have a tendency to bark more than others. Because most dogs live in houses close to other people who may be disturbed by the noise, it is important to teach dogs not to bark unnecessarily. Ignoring attention-seeking barking, calming an excited dog, and minimizing intruder-alert barking are key to good relations with neighbours, as well as for keeping your own stress levels low. Interrupt barking whenever it occurs, and calmly engage your dog in another activity. Ask him to come to you as soon as he has sounded the alarm if there is someone near the property.

◁ *Attention seeking*
If your dog looks at you when he barks, he is probably trying to get your attention. Make sure he has enough good-quality attention throughout the day and then ignore him completely if he barks at you.

△ *On guard*
Dogs bark at delivery people because they think they are doing something suspicious, such as pushing something through the letter box. Teach your dog to run to you for treats and games just before they arrive.

GOOD PRACTICE

Never encourage a young puppy to bark. Most dogs will bark naturally to alert their owners against intruders as they get more confident during adolescence. Encouragement will cause an over-reaction, which will become a nuisance.

Teaching your dog to bark is easy (right), but teaching him to be quiet (far right) is much more difficult. Only attempt this if you have already successfully trained him to perform lots of other exercises.

Teach "speak!"
Tease your dog with a toy while he is tied to a fixed object. Reward any slight noise he makes immediately with freedom, games, and praise. Eventually reward continuous barking.

Be quiet
When your dog barks, say "quiet" and give a hand signal. Wait for him to stop and then reward him immediately with praise and a treat. Practise doing this several times in the course of a short session.

Overexcitement
Some dogs bark when they are excited. Refuse to do anything until your dog is quiet. This will calm him down and teach him that barking does not achieve anything.

Accepting handling

Teaching your dog to accept handling will make him a better patient if he is ill or injured. It also builds a trusting bond between you, improving your relationship and making him feel more at ease when you touch him.

We like to touch and hold our dogs as a sign of our affection for them, but dogs do not touch each other unless they are fighting or mating. Accustoming your dog from an early age to being held, touched, lifted, and restrained teaches him that you are in control. It also makes it easier and more pleasant to carry out basic health checks, examine, groom, and bath him, clean his teeth, and clip his nails.

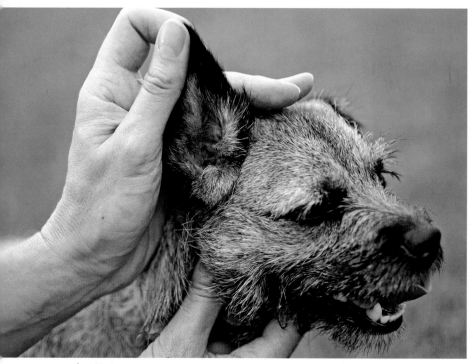

△ **Lift the ears**
Slowly lift your dog's ear flap to look inside. If this is too much for him, begin by slowly touching the ear and rewarding him well, progressing gradually to moving the ear.

▷ **Inspect the teeth**
Get your dog accustomed to lifting his top lip to look at the teeth. Holding his head, gently ease the side of the top lip back in order to expose the back teeth.

△ **Open the mouth**
Prise open the front teeth. Immediately let go and try for longer next time. Feed a treat quickly to make this a pleasant experience.

GOOD PRACTICE

If your dog looks anxious, nips at your fingers, or shows any other sign that he is unhappy with what you are doing, go more slowly and touch more gently. Relax him with gentle massages and stroking before trying again.

Touch
Humans like to touch, hold, and hug, but our dogs need to get used to this gradually, so they learn to accept and enjoy it eventually.

If your dog is unafraid but he wriggles and will not keep still, give him plenty of exercise before trying again.

Teach your dog to accept restraint by holding him tightly (although taking care not to cause him any discomfort) until he relaxes, then let him go immediately.

▷ **Touch the paws**
Paws are extremely sensitive, so touch them gently at first, working up to gentle paw squeezes later. Touch the nails with clippers and feed your dog a treat. This will help get him get used to having his nails trimmed in the future.

△ **Lift the tail**
Practise lifting your dog's tail gently. This will enable you to look underneath and will also get him accustomed to being touched in this area.

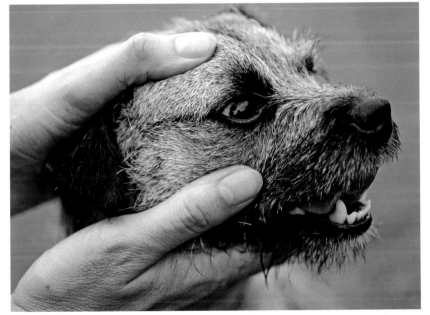

◁ **Examine the eyes**
With one thumb above the eye and the other positioned below, gently hold the eyelids apart so you can look in the eye. Be calm and patient. If your dog seems worried, slow down and hold the head steady first.

"**Humans** like to **touch,** hold, and hug, but **our dogs need to get used to this** gradually, so they **learn to accept** and **enjoy** it."

▷ **Lifting**
Lift your dog by placing one hand under his bottom to support his weight, then lifting under his chest with the other hand. Lift him slowly, so he feels secure, and bring him carefully in towards your body.

Doggy
dilemmas

Solving training problems

Solving training problems

It is easy to get stuck in the middle of a training session and reach a point where **your dog does not want to work,** or he **cannot seem to understand what you are asking him to do.** This section will give you ideas on what might be going wrong with your training, and advice on **how to fix these problems.** All of the common reasons for training difficulties are included here – find out what you need to know to **help you and your dog progress.** It also offers guidance on the thorny issue of **dog aggression,** with information on **where to get further help** if necessary.

OUT OF CONTROL
Dog training is not always easy, and we sometimes need help and advice to overcome the difficulties we are experiencing with our dogs.

Unrewarding rewards

Training using positive methods relies on your dog wanting the reward that is on offer. Knowing what your dog likes most, and guessing what he might want at the moment you wish to train him takes skill and practice.

Dogs make a choice between what they want to do and what we are asking them to do. The rewards you give need to match the task you are asking your dog to do, and also be valuable to him at that moment in time. If you are struggling to get your dog to respond, try increasing the value of the treats or games you are offering (pp.108–9), or give him something different.

◁ *Too much pressure*
A low-value treat, combined with too much pressure from the owner, can cause a dog to show no interest in working. Adopt a more relaxed approach and increase the value of the reward you are offering (p.108).

◁ *Have fun*
Having fun with your dog and building a good relationship will allow you to reward him with praise and approval, with only occasional treats and games to keep his responses sharp.

△ *Top choice*
Find out which treats or toys your dog values most highly, and use these only for complicated tasks and difficult exercises, and for when your dog would rather be doing something else.

"**Find out** which **treats or toys** your dog **values** most **highly.**"

◁ *Allow exploration*
Lack of interest in food or toys when outside may be due to excitement or anxiety. To teach your dog to overcome the distractions that a new area brings, allow him to explore a restricted area until it becomes familiar to him.

▷ *Focus*
Once your dog has had a chance to explore and relax, offer him a tasty treat or a game with a toy to regain his focus before you attempt further training. Repeated sessions like this will teach your dog to concentrate on you and training when outside.

GOOD PRACTICE

The unexpected is always more exciting and intriguing than the familiar, so keep your dog guessing as to what reward he is going to get, and offer something new if his performance is deteriorating.

Make sure that your dog understands your voice cues before you start to reduce the rewards you give him on a variable reinforcement schedule (pp.116–7). Jackpots must be both rewarding and fun.

You can make a new toy more valuable by keeping it to yourself and allowing your dog only brief and limited access for very good behaviour. This will make him work harder to get the reward.

Prize chew
Make a treat or game more rewarding by withholding it for a while and offering him something else instead.

Bad timing

If the timing of your rewards is not correct, your dog cannot learn what you are trying to teach. Rewarding actions immediately will ensure he does that same action again next time. Rewarding too late leads to training problems.

Rewarding immediately is the only way you have to let your dog know that he has done the correct action (pp.112–3), so make sure you always have rewards ready. Using a treat bag can help this, as treats are then close at hand. If your timing is too late, your dog will not know if he has done the right thing, and so will not learn what you want him to do. This can lead to confusion, frustration, and lack of interest in training for you both.

△ *Too little, too late*
If owners reward too late, the dog cannot see a reason for doing the action and quickly gets bored with trying. This can quickly result in a disinterested dog and a frustrated owner.

▷ *Getting it right*
To ensure you reward at the right time, concentrate on watching your dog carefully, getting your treat ready before you begin so that you can reward at the precise moment he does the required action. Have the treat to hand and feed immediately. Even if you have made a mistake and don't have the food ready, praise your dog warmly while you sort out the treat. Don't wait until he has moved on to thinking about other things.

△ *Reward the right action*
Be clear about what you are asking so that you can watch carefully for the action you require. Rewarding incorrect behaviour, such as dropping the toy outside the box instead of in the box, will result in your dog learning the wrong thing.

◁ *Reward small steps*
In the early stages of training, reward your dog for trying. Reward small approximations to the desired goal as soon as your dog tries, withholding the reward next time until he gives you more.

"**Concentrate** on watching your dog **carefully**. Have the **treat to hand** and feed immediately."

GOOD PRACTICE

Symptoms of bad timing are disinterest or frustration from the dog involved. If your dog tries to wander away during training sessions or barks with frustration, check your timing.

If your timing is out, you may succeed with easy exercises but may struggle with tasks that are quite complicated. If you cannot correct this by yourself, seek help from an experienced trainer who can show you how to get the timing right. Soon both you and your dog will be looking forward to training again.

Recognize the signs
If your dog walks off during a training session, it could be that your reward timing is off. Correct your timing, and you may see an improvement.

Make it easy

Dogs have less complex brains than humans and are less intelligent. Although it is tempting to treat them like children, we sometimes need to remember that they need help to understand what we mean.

To achieve success, you must make it easy for your dog to comply with your requests. Failure to do so can lead to confusion and a lack of response. Be prepared to go back a stage if necessary, and reward successful behaviour so he does it again next time.

△ **Help your dog**
This dog needs some help. The owner has asked for too much too soon and he cannot work out what is required of him. It is easy to get frustrated and think the dog is deliberately being disobedient.

▷ **Go back a stage**
Helping the dog out by going back a stage creates success and builds trust. Putting a sticky note on the cupboard door will trigger the right response, reminding him to shut it (pp.184–5).

△ **Make yourself clear**
This owner has asked the dog to bring a toy and calls him. The dog responds immediately to the call, temporarily forgetting about the toy. It is easy to think that the dog is being deliberately naughty.

> **"Helping your dog** out by **gently reminding** him what you want him to **do** results in **success."**

△ *Show him the toy*

Helping your dog by showing him what you wanted leads to success. Make sure you reward him well when he responds correctly, so that he remembers what to do next time you ask him to bring a toy back to you.

▷ *Reward success*

Rewarding only the behaviour that you want, once you have patiently helped your dog to understand what you require, ensures that it is more likely to happen next time you ask him to perform the same action.

GOOD PRACTICE

Always assume your dog is confused and does not understand what you want, rather than being disobedient, ignoring you on purpose, or just being stubborn.

If your dog will not do as you ask, check that he is well and wants what you are offering, and then go back to how you first trained the task and help him to understand what it is that you require.

Getting frustrated and angry when your dog fails to do as you ask is natural but undesirable. Instead, return to something he knows well and reward him for doing it. Then walk away, cool down, and go back to training when you have thought the exercise through more carefully.

Ignored?
If your dog is switching off, stop the lesson. Think of ways to make it easier for him to work out what you want him to do.

Dealing with **excess energy**

Young dogs and naturally lively breeds need plenty of exercise before they can concentrate on learning. Once your dog has released his excess energy, he will find it easier to focus on learning new tasks.

If your dog is boisterous and excitable, he will lack the ability to concentrate for long. Before a training session, it is a good idea to channel excess energy into a walk, a run, or vigorous play. The amount of time you need to spend exercising before training will depend on age and breed. Take care not to overexert your dog – you don't want him to be so tired that he's unwilling to participate in training.

◁ *Tire him out*
Before training exercises that are relatively sedentary and require your dog to be calm and peaceful – for example "settle" (pp.192–3) – make sure that he has had plenty of free running and games with toys to use up his excess energy.

▽ *Running free*
Free running is essential for lively and energetic dogs. Teach your dog to come back when called (pp.124–5), so that he can be allowed off the lead in safe areas.

> **"**Your dog's **energy levels** will depend on **age** and **breed."**

▽ *Losing interest*
Puppies have shorter attention spans, so lessons should be kept short. Don't expect your puppy to stay still for long, as his desire to move around is strong.

△ *Mind games*
Playing interesting games with toys is an excellent way to use up your dog's mental energy, as well as tiring him out physically. A young, lively dog will be more willing to work after play.

◁ *New tricks*
Older dogs can concentrate for longer and can go straight into lessons without the need for lots of running and energetic games beforehand.

GOOD PRACTICE

If your dog is easily distracted, and excitable and active – jumping up or nipping at your hands or toys, for example – you need to get rid of some of his energy before training him. Physical exercise from free running and games will tire him enough to concentrate.

Increase the amount of exercise your dog gets on every walk by playing games with him. Take toys on walks with you rather than throwing sticks for him to chase, which can be dangerous.

Stay in control
Freedom to run and play off the lead is essential for all dogs, but they must be under your control at all times and come back reliably when called.

Only behaves at home

Many dogs are well trained and behave perfectly at home, but seem naughty and disobedient elsewhere. This is a fault of the training, not the dog, and you should be aware that you need to train in all sorts of different situations.

Lack of familiarity with your cues can result in your dog failing to respond to your requests when you are away from home. Unfamiliar situations also bring distractions that entice your dog away from what you are asking him to do. Training all exercises from the beginning in many different places, using high-value treats, and with many repetitions, is the key to success.

◁ **Unsettled**
If your dog lies down and relaxes at home when you have visitors but will not do so at a friend's house, he needs further training. Make appointments to visit your friends, so you can practise. This will get him used to relaxing in other environments.

▽ **Selective deafness**
Running off on walks is common. Such dogs often come when called immediately at home but have not been trained to come back when distractions are present.

"**Dogs** who **do not respond** to cues away from home are **not 'naughty'**; they are **distracted.**"

"Be kind and patient. Train the exercises again in a wide range of places."

◁ **Practise on a line**
Patient teaching, using a long line to keep control, is required until your dog responds every time. Make sure you have high-value treats and practise until your dog is perfect.

△ **Confused**
Many dogs will not perform a well-learned trick in front of an audience. A different location and the presence of other people are enough to change the associations to such an extent that he will not know what you are asking.

△ **Back to basics**
If your dog cannot work out what to do, return to his basic training and make it easy for him to understand what you want. You will find that he soon remembers what to do, and eventually he will be able to respond correctly in many different environments.

GOOD PRACTICE

Dogs who do not respond to cues away from home are not "naughty"; they are just distracted or do not understand. In this case, there has been insufficient training in other locations (pp.114–5), and you need to train these exercises again in a wide range of conditions and places until your dog behaves well in all situations.

If your dog is anxious when he is away from home, it will naturally take him longer to respond to your requests, because he will be busy watching out for things that may seem threatening to him. Be kind and patient and try to help him get over his anxieties before asking him to do things for you (pp.156–7). In time, he should feel relaxed enough to respond.

New location
Training your dog in different environments is key to helping him feel relaxed and confident enough to perform in any situation.

Bad dog?
Solving training problems becomes easier
if you look at the world from your dog's
viewpoint to see what he finds rewarding.
Arrange situations so that he is rewarded
for doing what you want him to do instead.

Fear-based aggression

The main reason why dogs become aggressive is that they are afraid. Aggression may be the only way a dog knows to get the threat to move away. If a dog feels he is in extreme danger, he may even resort to biting.

Aggression towards people is usually reserved for suspicious strangers, but a dog may become aggressive towards his owner if he is being punished and if he is very frightened of the person. Most aggression towards other dogs is also fear-based. Dogs will usually show signs that they are scared first, but if this fails to protect them from the threat, and they have enough confidence, they will use aggression to keep themselves safe. Aggression usually escalates from growling to snapping to biting, but in some situations a dog may bite without giving any warning if he feels sufficiently scared.

▷ *"Go away!"*
Owners can find it difficult to believe that their dog's aggression has its origins in fear, as a dog does not look afraid when lunging or barking. However, it may have displayed fearful body language earlier and been ignored, forcing the dog to take this drastic action.

▽ *Cornered*
This dog is tied up, and he has no choice but to use aggression to confront the danger he faces. Most dogs do not want to bite, and will put up a good warning display to try to get the threat to back off.

◁ *Learning to fight*
Uncontrolled rough play can force the underdog to become aggressive in order to make the other dog stop. If successful, this behaviour is quickly learned and will be used in another similar situation.

△ *Muzzles*
Control measures are vital for aggressive dogs. Muzzles can help to keep people and other animals safe, but a muzzled dog can still harm. Good behavioural therapy is also needed.

◁ *Preventing aggression*
Socialize young puppies with everything they will encounter as adults (pp.92–3). Failure to do so will result in a dog that is scared and more likely to bite.

> " In some situations **a dog may bite without** giving any **warning** if he feels **scared enough.**"

GOOD PRACTICE

Keeping a good distance from things that you know scare your dog will minimize the chances of him becoming stressed. Move away as soon as you see the first signs of distress or fear (pp.74–5).

Never force a shy dog forward to "confront his fear". Appreciate that he is afraid, and try to help him to find a way to overcome his fears without forcing him.

Fear-based aggression is a serious issue, and you will need the help of an experienced pet behaviourist to help you and your dog overcome the problem. See p.254 for details of the relevant groups that can help you, or ask your veterinary surgeon to refer you. The pet behaviourist will work out a treatment plan for you to follow that will involve desensitization to the fear stimulus and counter-conditioning to replace bad feelings with good ones.

Shyness
Shy dogs are potential fear-biters if they find themselves in the wrong situation. They need gentle help to overcome their concerns.

Other causes of aggression

As well as fear, there are many other reasons why a dog may decide to fight or bite. Owners need to be aware of potential problems, and take action to prevent their dogs from feeling that aggression is the only option.

Dogs have no words to tell us when they are upset or to ask us to help them. Most dogs live peacefully with us and with each other, but they occasionally resort to aggression to get their own way or to make a point. Finding out why they feel like this is the key to solving the problem. Feeling protective towards food, fighting with other dogs for a place in the household hierarchy, or biting to avoid pain – such as the pain of a tail being trodden on – are just some of the reasons why dogs may be aggressive.

> **"** Dogs have **no words to tell us** when they **are upset** or to **ask us to help them. "**

◁ *"Mine!"*
Guarding food is a natural behaviour for dogs, whose ancestors needed to do so in order to prevent starvation. Aggression from us will make the problem worse. They need to be gently persuaded that we are no threat to their food.

▽ *"Watch it!"*
If your dog shows aggression towards other dogs, try to reduce opportunities for conflict. Do not let him off-lead, keep your distance from other dogs, and get him focused on you. Seek professional help (p.254) for a long-term solution.

▽ *"Leave it!"*

Fighting between two dogs that live in the same home is common, particularly when both animals are entire. Reinforcement of an existing hierarchy by the owners and neutering (pp.88–9) are possible solutions. A pet behaviourist can give you an independent assessment and a treatment plan (p.254).

▷ *"Ouch!"*

Sensitive dogs may find grooming painful and unpleasant, and use aggression to let their owners know this. Be gentle, so that your dog learns to trust that you won't hurt him. Brush slowly, taking care not to pull, and keep grooming sessions short.

GOOD PRACTICE

Whether a dog is feisty or likely to bite is determined, to a great extent, by his breed. Some breeds of dog can cope with many adverse circumstances before they react, whereas others are more easily provoked. How comfortable the dog feels physically can also have an effect, just as it can for us, and factors such as being too hot, too hungry, or too tired, can lower thresholds for aggression.

Many owners become aggressive in response to their dog's aggression. This only serves to escalate the aggression and ruin the relationship between dog and owner. Getting advice from an experienced pet behaviourist (p.254) will help you to find a solution for both of you.

Volatile
Terriers were bred to be courageous and feisty, so it is no surprise that many are quick to resort to aggression. Consequently, terriers need good socialization. They should be removed quickly from high-arousal situations.

Troubleshooting

Despite both good intentions and patient training sessions, sometimes dogs do not perform the desired action perfectly. Here are some examples of common training problems, with advice on how to solve them.

Doggy dilemmas

Q *My dog walks well on the lead when coming home from the park, but pulls all the way there. How can I prevent this?*

A He pulls on the lead to get to the park faster, so teach him that, instead, pulling results in slower progress – because you stop and make him wait. He needs to learn that if he keeps the lead loose, you will walk more quickly. Start this exercise (pp.134–5) from the moment you attach the lead to his collar so that you are training even as you go out of the door and down the path. It may take a long time to reach the park at first, but you will get faster with fewer stops each time you practise. Tire him out with some energetic games in the garden first to reduce his incentive to race to the park for exercise.

Q *I'm trying to teach my dog to jump while carrying a toy in his mouth, but he keeps dropping it. What should I do?*

A It is perfectly normal for dogs to forget to do one thing while concentrating on another. Teach jumping (pp.168–9) and retrieving (pp.136–41) separately for a while until your dog can do each task easily and without concentrating. Then ask him to do both at the same time. If he drops the toy before jumping, don't reward him but, instead, immediately take him back to the toy, ask him to "fetch" it again, and then ask him to jump again (keep the jump very low at first). You will have to keep repeating this gently until he gets it right, then praise him enthusiastically when he does.

Q *When I ask my dog to sit at a distance, he walks towards me and sits when he reaches me. How can I teach him to sit in the right place each time?*

A All previous rewards have been for putting his bottom on the ground when right next to you, so when you ask him to sit, he will try to do this again – which means he has to get to you first. Teach him that he will get his reward for sitting wherever he is (pp.152–3) by preventing him from moving towards you until he gets the idea. Don't get cross with him for walking towards you, or he will begin to creep forward slowly.

"Reward your dog well for **performing the right action."**

Q *My dog comes back to me with his toy but he won't give it up. What can I do?*

A Some dogs enjoy the possession of a toy just as much, or more, than the chase. Giving it up is hard for them because you are taking away something they enjoy (similar to someone taking money from you and not giving it back). Encourage your dog to give the toy to you by offering something he would rather have, such as food or a favourite toy. He may find it easier to drop the toy rather than allow you to take it from him. Teach him to trust that you will give it back once you have it by returning it to him or throwing it again for him to chase.

Q *When I ask my dog to play dead (pp.166–7), he rolls onto his back and wags his tail. How can I teach him to do what I want?*

A This is funny, so why not put it on cue so you can get him to do it again next time (pp.110–11)? When you want to teach the play dead trick, use a food lure to position your dog carefully, then give your reward in the form of social approval and laughter (pp.108–9), because this reaction has been so successful in the past. Reward the "dead" position quickly at first, and then gradually build up the time he must hold it before rewarding. If you leave it too long and he rolls onto his back and wags his tail, try not to laugh, but patiently lure him into the correct position again and reward well.

Troubleshooting

Q *I've tried to get my English Setter to play but he is not interested. What can I do?*

A Play has its origins in the rehearsal of hunting behaviour. Anything you can do with a toy that simulates a small, fast-moving creature will stimulate your dog to give chase. Tie a small piece of sheepskin onto a line and then weave it in and out of some long grass to tempt your dog to follow it and pounce. Keep moving it erratically, sometimes showing it to him and then, at other times, hiding it. Always be sure to stop the game before your dog gets bored, and then try again a little later. You will find that short, fun play sessions like this will build his interest and, gradually, can be turned into games with toys.

Q *My dog likes people so much he runs to them before coming back to me when I call. How can I teach him to come back?*

A The downside of having a well-socialized dog is that they like people so much that it is sometimes very difficult to stop them greeting anyone and everyone they encounter when out on a walk. To train your dog to check in with you first (pp.150–1), use a long line, but take care not to get tangled in it or trip anyone else up. Use this to reel your dog back to you gently whenever he sees someone he wants to greet. Always reward him really well for coming back, even if you had to make it happen, and then allow him to greet the person in a controlled way if you think it is appropriate.

"Allow him to greet the person in a controlled way."

Q *My dog won't "go to bed" when visitors come. How can I teach him to do this?*

A The rewards you are offering your dog for going to his bed do not outweigh the rewards he gains by being sociable with visitors. Therefore you must either step up the rewards he receives for being on his bed – perhaps by giving him a tasty chew – or accept that he wants to be sociable and train him to behave politely with visitors instead. You could also try waiting until the excitement of having visitors has died down before asking your dog to go to his bed, to increase the likelihood of a positive response from him. Alternatively, gently insist that he does as you ask, using a house line to make sure that it happens (pp.118–9).

"Give him a **tasty chew… or train him** to **behave politely.**"

Q *When I ask my dog to fetch the lead, he will bring anything he can find before eventually bringing his lead. How can I teach him to respond correctly to me first time?*

A Take these things from him but do not give him any reward. When he does bring you the lead, praise him really well. In this way, he will soon learn that there is no reward for picking up other things. To make it easier, go back to training him with only the lead in view (pp.178–9) until he understands the word for this action, and then add another item and help him to make the right decision.

Q *I like to go for a walk with my friend and her dog but my dog pulls on the lead so much that it is not enjoyable. How can I stop him doing this?*

A Train your dog to walk well on a loose lead in all situations (pp.132–5). When he is reliable, enlist your friend's help and bring your dogs together for training. Ask her to walk around you in a big circle while you train your dog to walk beside you. Practise this until he walks calmly at your side. Then walk in parallel with the other dog and practise again, with your friend walking very slowly, so he does not get too far ahead.

6

Out and **about**

Sports and fun

Sports and fun

Dog sports provide excitement and fun for both dog and owner. There are many to choose from, and finding one that suits you both will result in many hours of shared pleasure. **Use the exercises in the preceding chapters** to train your dog to understand and respond to numerous cues, which will lay the foundations for taking part. Dog sports provide a **framework for further training,** help you to learn **new skills,** and make an **enjoyable hobby** in the process. The **wide variety of canine sports** available are described here, along with **advice on how to get involved,** and **how you and your dog can get fit** for the activity you have chosen.

WATER RETRIEVES
Dogs love to swim once they know how to do so, and it is a good way for them to get fit without risking injury.

Getting involved

Sporting activities involving dogs are fun. There are many to choose from, and your dog will love the excitement and exercise. Each sport will give you a different perspective on training, and increase your skills.

Once you have completed the basic training given in previous chapters, you and your dog will be ready to start training for one of the many dog sports available. Dog sports give you aims and goals to train for, and really improve your training ability and knowledge. They enable you to make new friends who have a similar interest and, when you reach competition stage, will take you to many different parts of the country that you haven't visited before. If you use only positive training methods and make sure your training sessions are always fun for your dog, he will love taking part, too. Participating in

△ **Star performer**
Sociable dogs enjoy the attention, activity, and performance of dog sports, and revel in the atmosphere of shows and competitions.

a dog sport will provide him with exercise and a chance to use his mental energy. He will get fitter and smarter, and the bond between you will get stronger. There is nothing like working in partnership with your dog to achieve goals, especially when you win your class.

▷ **Agility**
Both owners and dogs need to be fit and supple to make turns at high speed on agility courses. The jumps are lowered for smaller dogs to make the competition fair.

"Your dog will get **fitter** and **smarter,** and the **bond between you** will get **stronger."**

◁ **Gun dog scurry**
Country fairs often have competition scurries to test the working ability of gun dogs. These events are informal and organizers sometimes allow other breeds to participate.

▽ **Cani-cross**
Energetic owners can take part in sports that require as much effort from them as from their dog. Dogs and owners need to get fit gradually.

▷ **Flyball**
Pressing a pedal to release a ball is an essential flyball skill. All breeds can take part, although fast, active dogs are usually the winners.

Practice is vital

Practice is the secret to success in dog sports. During competitions, handlers get nervous; dogs pick up on those emotions and their performance suffers. The only way to overcome this is to make responses to cues so automatic that nothing affects them. This is done by repeated practice until responses are perfect. Training at home is essential for this and finding a place to practise and any necessary equipment is important if you want to be placed. Training sessions need to be frequent, because the total number of hours you put in will make the difference between failure and success.

Which sport?

Decide which sport seems most appealing to you. Pages 234–45 will give you an outline of the most popular ones, but there are others that are less common. What you decide to get involved in usually depends on what is available in your area. Be prepared to travel to learn the skills required, and particularly to take part in competitions held around the country. To find out more about these sports, trawl the internet, contact the Kennel Club (p.254), and buy magazines dedicated to dogs. Most competitions are registered with the Kennel Club, so get in touch to find out where to go and watch. Talk to competitors after they have competed to learn more.

To know what is available in your area, watch out for advertisements for shows and courses in local vets' offices, pet shops, or food-supply merchants. Ask local dog-care professionals such as veterinary surgery staff, groomers, or dog-walkers about the various clubs in your area. The Kennel Club may have a list of the larger clubs, but it won't be comprehensive.

If there are no clubs in your area for your chosen sport, attend a beginner's course. These are often advertised on websites. The standard of teaching will vary, so it is a good idea to ask at shows for names of teachers who will put you on the right path from the outset.

Get fit for sport

Dog sports require dogs and owners to be fit and ready for the physical challenges ahead. Getting into shape takes time and effort, and needs to be done slowly to allow bodies time to adapt.

Preparation

All dog sports are active and energetic, and will require your dog to be healthy and physically fit. Unless you already have a very active lifestyle, it will be necessary to build up your dog's fitness, strength, and stamina gradually so that he can cope with the rigours of his new sport without injuring himself.

▽ ▷ **Slimming down**
Overweight pets (right) struggle to run, jump, and play, and tire easily. They need to be slimmed down gradually by reducing food intake and increasing exercise until they are the correct weight (below).

Different sports require different physical abilities, and you will need to check carefully what is necessary with experts in your chosen sport. They will also be able to give you some valuable tips on how to achieve this level of fitness and help you plan a realistic schedule. Before any exercise schedule is started, your dog needs to be the correct weight (pp.78–9). If your dog is overweight, reduce his weight by cutting down the amount of food you give him and increasing his exercise. It is really important to reduce weight gradually, because sudden changes can be damaging and distressing to your dog. Check with your veterinary surgeon before starting a weight loss plan.

"**New sporting activities** will use different **muscle groups** than you and **your dog** have used previously."

△ ▷ **Play exercise**
Playing with toys is an easy way to get your dog fit. Teach retrieve so your dog brings the ball back to you, but do not run him until he is exhausted.

In addition, a fit dog needs a fit handler, so don't neglect your own fitness programme. Remember that both of you need to warm up gradually before undertaking any strenuous physical activity.

Building strength

New sporting activities will use different muscle groups than you and your dog have used previously. It will take time for these muscles to develop sufficiently to allow both of you to do the sport easily. Asking your dog to jump repeatedly, or to fetch a Frisbee over and over when he is not used to it will make him stiff and sore. For this reason, curb your enthusiasm and remember

△ **Jogging**
Jogging with your dog is good exercise and improves stamina. You are putting in as much effort as your dog, so it is easy to know when to stop.

that it is your dog who is putting in all the effort! Try to plan your sessions in advance so that you set a limit on how many repetitions of a particular action you will do each day.

Increasing stamina

Some sports require your dog to have lots of stamina and to keep going for hours – sometimes days – before resting. Many breeds are capable of this, but all need time to build up their stamina gradually before performing at a high level.

▷ **Fit for life**
Dog sports keep both dogs and handlers supple, strong, healthy, and fit. Building up gradually to this point will help prevent injuries.

Because your dog cannot tell you when he has had enough, and most dogs will not want to stop while their owner is still ready for more, it is important to plan a steady, stamina-building programme, with the help of more experienced people in the sport and your veterinary surgeon. Gradually increasing stamina takes time, but will save injuries and breakdowns through ill health later by slowly strengthening muscles and tendons.

Agility

Sometimes referred to as "showjumping for dogs", canine agility is a sport that involves skill and speed, requiring dogs to tackle a wide variety of obstacles. Increasingly popular, it is great fun for you and your dog.

Loved by dogs and owners alike, canine agility is a sport of skill, action, and fun. Dogs learn to negotiate different obstacles, and once they have learned how to tackle each piece of equipment, they begin to run courses against the clock. In competitions, dogs negotiate courses of varying degrees of difficulty, and the fastest and most accurate in each class wins. Most elements of agility can be practised at home with the minimum of equipment. However, joining a club is essential to enable you to grasp the intricacies of each obstacle, and to give you a chance to learn on equipment that you are unlikely to have at home, such as the dog walk and A-frame.

A good training class and club will also encourage you and help you to find out all the essential information needed to compete. It is important that dogs are physically mature before they begin training. Growing bones and joints can be damaged by jumping at an early age, so puppies should not be encouraged to jump until they are 12 months old. Dogs are not allowed to compete in agility until they are 18 months of age.

▽ **Learning jumps**
Jumping can be taught and practised at home. Smaller jumps are set up for "mini dogs" to make it fair when they compete against bigger dogs.

"Dogs learn to negotiate different obstacles. Once they learn each piece of equipment, they run courses against the clock."

△ **Learning tunnels**
Tunnels may need to be shortened at first to encourage dogs to go through, but, like this West Highland Terrier, they soon gain confidence if the training is taken slowly.

The hoop
The hoop is suspended on a frame. Dogs need to learn to judge the height accurately so they can sail through.

▷ **Tunnels**
Tunnels can be straight or bent, rigid or made of canvas. Once dogs have mastered them, they travel through them at such a rate that the tunnel needs to be pegged down to keep it stable.

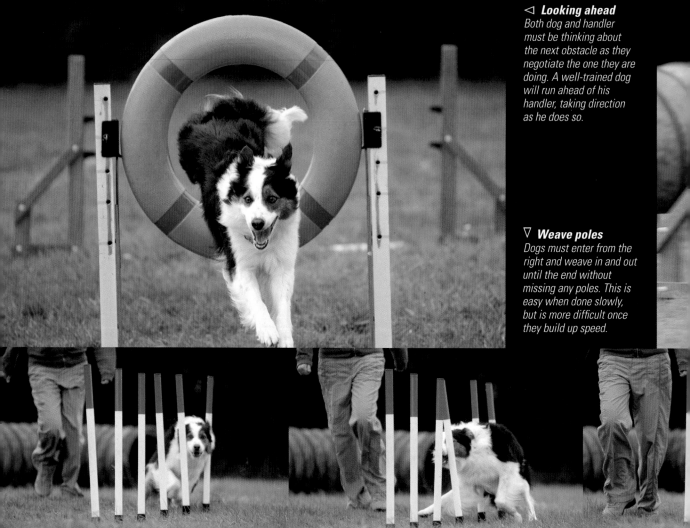

◁ **Looking ahead**
Both dog and handler must be thinking about the next obstacle as they negotiate the one they are doing. A well-trained dog will run ahead of his handler, taking direction as he does so.

▽ **Weave poles**
Dogs must enter from the right and weave in and out until the end without missing any poles. This is easy when done slowly, but is more difficult once they build up speed.

△ **See-saw**
The see-saw is pivoted and dogs learn to run up and tip the balance using their weight. They have to touch the yellow contact points at both ends with their feet, so they need to be accurate as well as fast.

◁ **Jumps**
Accuracy during jumping is required for competitions, and points are lost if jumps are knocked down. The course has many twists and turns, and it is easy to knock jumps down by cutting corners too fine.

▷ **Perfect Harmony**

This dog and its owner are in time, in harmony, having fun, and on show. This image epitomizes the sport of freestyle – you can almost hear the music. As with all performances, many hours of rehearsal are the key to success.

▽ **Essential routines**

Routines are taught piece by piece, and practised until they are perfect. Each part must be performed with speed and accuracy. Only then are they put together into sequences and, finally, set to music.

Freestyle and heelwork to music, otherwise known as dancing with dogs, is tremendously popular. It combines rehearsed movements choreographed to music to present a polished performance – great fun for dogs and owners.

Heelwork to music was developed in the early 1990s in the UK to show the public how interesting heelwork can be, and it spread rapidly around the world. The sport gradually developed, and freestyle was created out of a desire to demonstrate other manoeuvres, in which the dog moves out of the heelwork position – for example, to move away from the handler, to jump, twist, and walk on two legs. Freestyle is more exciting to watch than heelwork, and is now the more popular choice of competition. Competitors are given four minutes to demonstrate their routines to the music of their choice. They are judged on programme content (a greater variety of moves gains more marks), on accuracy and execution of movement, and on musical interpretation.

▷ **Anything goes**
Freestyle allows props, such as skipping ropes, canes, hoops, and hats, to be used to help display more elaborate routines. A wide variety of manoeuvres makes the performance more interesting, and will earn more marks.

Many training clubs now offer courses for beginners and the sport's popularity makes it fairly easy to find a course to help you get started. All training is by reward and encouragement, as it is nearly impossible to make dogs do some of the moves if they don't want to. For this reason, both dogs and owners enjoy the training, and experienced dogs get very excited when they hear the music for their session.

Freestyle is open to any breed of dog and any age of handler. It suits dogs who enjoy the repetition and level of activity needed for the many rehearsals required, and suits

handlers with a sense of rhythm. Both dog and handler need to be physically fit and supple for this sport. The movements are easy to teach, but a basic level of obedience is required before you begin; it is an advantage to have a good working partnership already established. Working through the exercises in this book (pp.122–85) provides the perfect foundation for this training.

"**Dogs** as well as owners **enjoy** the **training**, and **experienced dogs** get very **excited** when they **hear the music** for their **session**."

Flyball

Flyball is fun, furiously energetic, and intensely exciting. Teams of dogs race each other, jumping small hurdles to reach a flyball box that delivers a ball they must catch before jumping the hurdles again to return to their handlers.

Flyball is a relatively new sport that originated in California in the 1960s. Due to its popularity, it has spread rapidly around the world.

The flyball box is a machine that fires a tennis ball into the air when a dog presses the pedal. The dog has to run to the box via a series of four hurdles, jumping these along the way, then press the pedal of the box, which releases the ball.

The dog has to catch the ball and then carry it back over the hurdles to the handler.

Once the first dog is back, the second dog is released, and so on, until all four dogs in the team have run. If a dog faults – for example, by running outside the jumps, or failing to return the ball – it must run again until it gets it right. The team cannot finish until all dogs have run correctly, and the first team with all dogs back successfully is the winner. Competitions are run as a series of heats, with the winners of early heats running against other winners, until eventually there are two teams left for the final.

Flyball is a great spectator sport, as well as being fun for competing dogs and owners. Any active dog can take part and the training is relatively easy. The most difficult part of training is trying to stop dogs taking the quickest route, which is down the side of the jumps rather than over them.

This sport suits sociable owners who enjoy the camaraderie of being part of a team, and is great for active dogs who enjoy retrieving.

> **"Flyball** is a great **spectator sport** as well as being **fun** for **competing dogs** and **owners."**

△ **Jumping the hurdles**
All jumps are painted white and many are padded in case a dog accidently makes contact with them. During training, "wings" are used to prevent the dogs from going around the hurdles instead of over them.

▷ **The flyball box**
There are many different varieties of flyball boxes. Some launch the ball into the air when the dog presses a pedal, while others allow dogs to run up a padded board and pick up the ball as they turn around.

Flyball fun
Dogs enjoy the speed, excitement, and activity of their run. The most successful dogs are fast and accurate, but spectators love the moment when dogs miss out jumps or drop the ball.

Obedience and Working Trials

Obedience and Working Trials are two serious sports. Both have entry via lower stakes that are easier for dog and handler. These sports are for serious trainers who enjoy the rewards a true working partnership brings.

Obedience

Rules and exercises vary between countries, but all have easier stakes for beginners – gradually getting more difficult as dog and handler progress to the higher levels. Obedience exercises include heelwork on- and off-lead, recall, stays, and retrieve. Higher classes may require drop on recall, jumping, a send-away, distance control, and a scent-discrimination exercise.

Obedience clubs are easily found and will help beginners to get started. Be sure to find ones that use positive training methods where dogs and owners are having fun and learning easily. This sport is very competitive and dogs will need to be prepared to a high level.

In obedience competitions, movements must be precise and accurate to earn marks. Points are won or lost on the movement of a paw, so this sport suits people who pay attention to detail and accuracy.

Working Trials

Working trials consist of exercises similar to those used to train police dogs, although "man work" is only taught at the highest levels. Dogs and handlers progress through five stakes, qualifying at both open and championship shows before moving on to the next stage. Exercises are divided into three sections:

■ Nose work involves following a track about 2.4km (1.5 miles) long, and recovering two objects laid on it. The other component of nose work is to search a marked area, recovering any articles in it that carry human scent.

■ Agility requires the dog to clear a 1m (3ft) hurdle, a 1.8m (6ft) scale, and a 2.7m (9ft) long jump.

■ The control round involves heelwork, send-away, retrieving, stays, steadiness to gunshot, and speak on command.

△ **Obedience heelwork**
Heelwork for competitions needs to be close and precise. Points are deducted if any gap appears between a dog and its handler.

▷ **Retrieve**
The dumbbell retrieve is common in both competitions. In obedience, retrieve, delivery, present, and finish must be precise. Crooked sits or mouthing will lose marks.

▷ **Long jump**
It may look like a long way, but most dogs clear the long jump easily. Although it consists of separate units, the jump is designed to look solid from the dog's perspective before take-off.

△ **Tracking**
The dog follows a track of scents produced by crushed vegetation, disturbed earth, skin cells, and clothing particles left by the track-layer. Track conditions such as wind, rain, dryness, and ground temperature affect the dog's performance.

◁ **The scale**
A dog has to wait until told to go, then must scale the jump, land on the other side, and wait until recalled by his owner. Dogs can be injured by repeated landings from such a height unless they are very fit.

Gun dog work

Gun dog work, field trial competitions, and working tests remain the preserve of gun dog breeds – other types of dogs are not allowed. Gun dogs are among the few breeds that are still used for their original purpose.

Gun dog field trials and working tests are usually held in the summer months and use only canvas dummies instead of real game. For the rest of the year, gun dogs are needed on live shoots and for hunting.

If you find the idea of shooting and dispatching game distasteful, then field trials are preferable to real gun dog work, where birds or animals will be shot around you.

Field trials are run predominantly to check on a dog's ability to do the real work of a gun dog, and so you will come into contact with people who take pleasure in hunting.

Field trials and tests are designed to resemble, as much as possible, a day's shooting in the field, and all aspects of the dog's capabilities will be tested. The gun dog breeds can be divided into retrievers, spaniels, pointers and setters, and

△ **Dummy run**
Canvas dummies, weighing about the same as a game bird, are used as a substitute for the real thing during field trials and working tests.

"hunt, point, and retrieve" breeds (HPRs). There are separate working tests for each of these groups, which are competitive in an informal way.

Gun dog field trials and tests are a great way to discover your dog's potential and will give you something to aim for with your training. This work is easy for gun dogs bred specifically for the purpose, and the most difficult thing is keeping control when they are doing something they love to do.

> "**Gun dog field trials** and **tests** are a great way to **discover your dog's potential,** and will give you **something to aim for.**"

◁ Pointing
Pointers and setters are used to locate birds for shooting and to indicate silently to the hunter by standing in this familiar posture. A dog should do this until the hunter signals he is ready, then the dog should scare the bird into the air.

△ Flushing
Spaniels are used for flushing game towards guns. They are busy and active, running continuously, scenting out birds, and scaring them into the air. Different varieties of spaniel have different roles: some are bred to work in thick cover, others for open ground or water.

△ Retrieving
Retrieving game from water takes strength and stamina. Dogs must have a strong possessive drive so that they will swim a long way to fetch a fallen bird. They must also be agreeable enough to give it up to the handler on their return.

▷ Control
Shooting can be hazardous, and it is important that gun dogs are under control at all times. Gun dogs must work as instructed, not do as they please. They must have a strong desire to work, but also entirely willing to take direction.

Other sports

As well as the more popular dog sports, there are a lot of less well-known ones in which you can participate. Which sport is right for you depends on the dog you have, your personal preference, and your capabilities.

The less well-known dog sports are sometime restricted, depending on which breed of dog you have. Only Afghan Hounds can take part in Afghan Hound racing, for instance, and it is usually only Newfoundlands and their crosses that are suitable for water work, Bloodhounds that take part in Bloodhound tracking tests, and Bernese Mountain Dogs that go carting.

Other sports are open to all dogs, but entries are sometimes restricted by ability and fitness. For example, only the most active of dogs can take part in bike- or ski-joring or sled-dog racing. Similarly, only certain people have the physical capacity to take part in demanding sports, such as cani-cross or dog hiking. Which sport you choose for you and your dog is a matter of what suits you

both, as well as personal preference. Your choice also depends, to some extent, on which sports are available in the area you live in. However, if you are very keen on a sport, there is always a way to do it. Although it is undeniably difficult to go ski-joring if you live in an area with no snow, you can go bike-joring instead if you can find roads and tracks nearby that are suitable.

◁ **Disc dog**
Disc-dog competitions involve a dog catching a Frisbee over increasingly larger distances. There is also a freestyle competition, where owner and dog can weave routines into their throwing and catching to earn more marks.

> "Which sport is **right** for **you** and **your dog** is a matter of **what suits** you both, and personal **preference.**"

△ **Newfoundland rescue**
Newfoundlands excel at water rescue. At special clubs, they learn to retrieve articles from the water, progressing to the more difficult task of rescuing people and boats.

◁ **Afghan Hound racing**
This is a fun sport for owners who like to see their dogs run and want to give them the opportunity to race in a safe place. The dogs are muzzled to prevent any injuries during the times of high excitement.

◁ ▽ **Joring**
The art of staying on a bike or skis while being pulled by dogs has developed into an organized sport. Dogs are harnessed and attached via a tow-line. It's great for dogs who love to run!

△ **Protection sports**
Protection sports such as *Schutzhund* ("protection dog") are popular with serious trainers. Reputable clubs avoid teaching unwanted aggression.

▷ **Dog hiking**
Dog hiking is for less competitive owners who enjoy active long walks with their dogs.

△ **Cani-cross**
In cani-cross, competitors run attached to their dog (or dogs) over a timed cross country course. Various levels are available to allow for all fitness levels and abilities.

Sled dogs
Huskies are the fastest, most efficient sled dogs, as they were purpose bred for this task. Other types of dog also enjoy the thrill of running fast over long distances, and can easily be trained to participate.

Index

Contents

Contacts

UK

DOG AND PUPPY TRAINING

Dog and puppy training classes, or individual tuition, can help you to progress more rapidly and assist with any individual difficulties. Choose someone experienced and knowledgeable, who uses only positive methods with both dogs and their owners. Other good sources of information about local trainers are local vets, dog wardens, groomers, and pet shops.

The following are useful organizations to contact when looking for a dog or puppy trainer:

Association of Pet Dog Trainers (national listings of pet dog trainers)
www.apdt.co.uk
E-mail: APDToffice@aol.com
Tel: 01285 810811
APDT, PO Box 17, Kempsford, GL7 4WZ

Puppy School (UK network of puppy trainers)
www.puppyschool.co.uk
E-mail: info@puppyschool.co.uk
PO Box 186, Chipping Norton, OX7 3XG

BEHAVIOUR PROBLEMS

If you are experiencing behaviour problems with your dog, it is best to get help fast before habits become too established. Look for someone with both practical experience and academic knowledge. They should work on veterinary referral, and be insured. Contact the Association of Pet Behaviour Counsellors or ask your veterinary surgeon to refer you to someone they trust.

Association of Pet Behaviour Counsellors
www.apbc.org.uk
Email: info@apbc.org.uk
Tel: 01386 751151

SOURCES OF NEW DOGS AND PUPPIES

As well as breeders, reputable rescue organizations are a good source of new puppies and adult dogs. Try to find a centre where they make the effort to assess all the dogs in their care so you can choose one to suit your temperament and lifestyle.

The following are useful organizations to contact when looking for a new dog or puppy:

The Battersea Dogs and Cats Home
www.battersea.org.uk
Tel: 020 7622 3626
4 Battersea Park Road, London, SW8 4AA

Dogs Trust
www.dogstrust.org.uk
Tel: 020 7837 0006
17 Wakley Street, London, EC1V 7RQ

Royal Society for the Prevention of Cruelty to Animals
www.rspca.org.uk
Tel: 0300 1234 555
RSPCA Enquiries Service, Wilberforce Way, Southwater, Horsham, West Sussex RH13 9RS.

Blue Cross
www.bluecross.org.uk
Tel: 01993 822651
Shilton Road, Burford, Oxon OX18 4PF

For further information on dog sports or breeders with puppies, contact:

The Kennel Club
www.thekennelclub.org.uk
Tel: 0870 606 6750
The Kennel Club, 1-5 Clarges Street, Piccadilly, London, W1J 8AB

USA

DOG AND PUPPY TRAINING

Dog and puppy training classes, or individual tuition, can help you to progress more rapidly and assist with any individual difficulties. Choose someone experienced and knowledgeable, who uses only positive methods with both dogs and their owners. Other good sources of information about local trainers are local vets, dog wardens, groomers, and pet shops.

The following are useful organizations to contact when looking for a dog or puppy trainer:

The Association of Pet Dog Trainers
www.apdt.com
E-mail: information@apdt.com
Tel: 1-800-PET-DOGS
(1-800-738-3647)
150 Executive Center Drive Box 35, Greenville, SC 29615

National Association of Dog Obedience Instructors
www.nadoi.org
PMB 369
729 Grapevine Hwy, Hurst, Texas 76054-2085, USA

BEHAVIOUR PROBLEMS

If you are experiencing behaviour problems with your dog, it is best to get help fast before habits become too established. Look for someone with both practical experience and academic knowledge. They should work on veterinary referral, and be insured. Contact the following organizations or ask your veterinary surgeon to refer you to someone they trust:

The International Association of Animal Behavior Consultants
www.iaabc.org
E-mail: info@iaabc.org
IAABC
565 Callery Road, Cranberry Township, PA 16066

Animal Behavior Society
http://www.animalbehavior.org/ABSAppliedBehavior/caab-directory

SOURCES OF NEW DOGS AND PUPPIES

As well as breeders, reputable rescue organiations are a good source of new puppies and adult dogs. Try to find a centre where they make the effort to assess all the dogs in their care so you can choose one to suit your temperament and lifestyle. The following are useful organizations to contact when looking for a new dog or puppy:

American Society for the Prevention of Cruelty to Animals (ASPCA)
www.aspca.org
Tel: (212) 876-7700
424 E. 92nd St, New York, NY 10128-6804

The Humane Society of the United States
www.hsus.org
Tel: 202-452-1100
2100 L St., NW, Washington, DC 20037

For further information on dog sports or breeders with puppies, contact:

American Kennel Club
www.akc.org
Tel: 919.233.9767
AKC Customer Care
8051 Arco Corporate Drive, Suite 100, Raleigh, NC 27617-3390

Acknowledgments

The author would like to thank the following: All those who have so kindly and willingly contributed to my knowledge of dog training and behaviour, including John Rogerson, Ian Dunbar, the late John Fisher, Tony Orchard, Carla Nieuwenhuizen, and many, many others. I would also like to thank Bobs Broadbent and Kris Glover who helped organize dogs and people for the photos when I couldn't be there. Thank you, also, to Victoria Wiggins of Dorling Kindersley for her expertise and patience, especially when I was losing mine. And finally, I would like to thank the dogs, those I have known and loved (particularly my beautiful Spider who appears in so many of the pictures in this book), those I have tried to help, and those who I've had fun with throughout my life. Without what I have learned from them, this book could never have been written.

Dorling Kindersley would like to thank the following:
Colour retouching: Craig Laker
Additional help: Simon Murrell
Additional design: Yenmai Tsang
Illustrations: Richard Tibbits

Also, Bobs Broadbent and Kris Glover, David Summers, Margaret and David Godel, Brad Murray and Jenny Woodcock, MDS Shows and Paws in the Park, Rachel Tooby and all the staff and dogs at Battersea Dogs and Cats Home, Old Windsor Branch.

And those who modelled in the book:
Sandra Alden, Laura Andrews
Lucy Avery, Gwen Bailey
Graham Bates, L. R. Bird
Sara Bradford, Bobs Broadbent
Savanagh Bryant, Alice Bungay
Tracy Bungay, Shelly Bushell
Ben Carlin, Lily Carlin
Nicky Carlin, Pen Carlin
Siobhan Dawson, Michael Donnelly
Deborah Duguid Farrant
Daniel Eaton, Helen Gardom
Kristina Glover, Wendy Grantham
Nala Gunstone, Elaine Hale
Emma Hugo, Jeremy Hugo
Sophie Hugo, Frances Johnstone
Ali Kaye, Sally Knight, Luca Lawrence
Poppy Lawrence, Tracy Lawrence
Alistair Lion, Kate Lye, Harriet
Mackevicius, Marika Marsh
Caroline Mooty, Jamie Mooty
Patrick Mooty, Iona Morris, Wil Morris
Elizabeth Munsey, Wendy Murphy,
Nicolette O'Neill, Phil Ormerond,
Ruth O'Rourke, Alice Peacock
Claire Pearson, Charlotte Pimm
David Roberts, Jessica Ryan-Ndegwa
Sebastian Ryan-Ndegwa, Joanne
Summers, Rob Symonds, Ian Tautz
Siân Thomas, Peter Thompson
Dawn Thorne, James Thorne
Marie Travers, Sarah Tyzack
Sophie von Maltzahn, Julie Warner
Esme Waters, Victoria Wiggins
Tomoko Wingate, Nigel Wright

Thank you to all the dogs whose photographs appear in this book:
Andy, Archie, Barney, Bella, Ben, Bertha, Billy, Blue, Bongo, Boris, Casha, Charlie Chesil, Coco, Dave, Diesel, Dotty, Fidget, Fin, Fizz, Gus, Harvey, Hero, Hoola, Jack, Jake, Jess, Jessie, Lettie, Libby, Lily, Lola, Maisie, Millie, Moojah, Morgan, Nuba, Otto, Ozzy, Penny, Q, Rosie, Sasuke, Scally, Scamps, Shep, Skipper, Spencer Spider, Talula, Thomas, Tink, Toby, Tom, Topsy, Walter, Zorro

Picture credits

The publisher would like to thank the following for their kind permission to reproduce the photographs:
l=left, r=right, t=top, c=centre, a=above, b=below.

18 Alamy Images: Dave Porter (bc). **FLPA:** Mike Lane (cr). **36 Getty Images:** Altrendo (br). **38 FLPA:** Imagebroker/Stefanie Krause-Wieczorek (clb). **39 Alamy Images:** Duravitski (bl). **Corbis:** Jim Craigmyle (br). **42 Alamy Images:** Juniors Bildarchiv (cla). **Corbis:** Sygma/Yves Forestier (tr). **52 Corbis:** Reuters/You Sung-Ho (br). **71 Alamy Images:** WoodyStock (c). **210 Corbis:** Lynda Richardson (br). **FLPA:** Erica Olsen (c). **212 Getty Images:** Iconica/Michael Cogliantry (cl). **223 Alamy Images:** Arco Images GmbH (c); PetStockBoys (t). www.chillpics.co.uk/www.canix. co.uk: Shane Wilkinson (cr). **236 FLPA:** Imagebroker/Alexander Trocha (cl). **Still Pictures:** Biosphoto/Klein J. & Hubert M.-L. (bc) (br). **237 Rex Features:** Keystone USA/SB. **240 FLPA:** Imagebroker/Thorsten Eckert (br). **241 Alamy Images:** Ashley Cooper (bl); SHOUT (cr). **Still Pictures:** Biosphoto/ Klein J. & Hubert M.-L. (tr). **243 Alamy Images:** Arco Images GmbH (c); Daniel Dempster Photography (tr). **FLPA:** Minden Pictures/Mark Ray Croft (tl). **244 Photolibrary:** Juniors Bildarchiv (bl) (bc) (br). **Rex Features:** Ken McKay (t). **245 Alamy Images:** Sherab (cr). **Photolibrary:** Juniors Bildarchiv (bl) (bc) (br). **246 Alamy Images:** blickwinkel (br); Shaun Flannery (bl). **Getty Images:** Stone/Sven Jacobsen (cl). **247 Alamy Images:** Ultimate Group, LLC (bc). **iStockphoto.com:** Rolf Klebsattel (clb). **PA Photos:** AP Photo/ Lewiston Sun Journal, Jose Leiva (tr). **Rex Features:** Newspix/Jody D'arcy (tl). www.chillpics.co.uk/www.canix.co.uk: Shane Wilkinson (br). **248-249 Photolibrary:** Joel Sheagren

All other images © Dorling Kindersley
For further information see:
www.dkimages.com

"Training is a life-long process. Keep finding time for training sessions, make them fun for both of you, and you will have a well-behaved dog for life." Gwen Bailey